AMERICA   S0-BJL-049
QUARTERLY

MONOGRAPH SERIES

Edited by NICHOLAS RESCHER

WITHDRAWN

STUDIES IN ONTOLOGY

Essays by:

Bas C. van Fraassen
R. M. Martin
Gerald J. Massey
Nicholas Rescher

Monograph No. 12   Oxford, 1978

PUBLISHED BY BASIL BLACKWELLL

© *American Philosophical Quarterly 1978*
ISBN 0 631 11560 9

111
SA9
105217
June 1978

PRINTED IN ENGLAND
by J. W. Arrowsmith Ltd., Bristol, BS3 2NT

CONTENTS

EDITOR'S PREFACE

In the spring of 1976 a consortium of scholarly organizations sponsored an International Philosophy Conference convened at the Biltmore Hotel in New York City, with the Philosophy Department of Baruch College of the City University of New York acting as host. One session of these meetings was a symposium on "Existence and Logic" with W. V. Quine in the role of discussant. The four essays presented in this APQ Monograph are somewhat revised versions of the principal papers delivered in this session. The editor is grateful to the participants for agreeing to this means for putting their papers before a wider audience. And he wishes to thank Professor Parviz Morewedge for facilitating arrangements both for the symposium and its publication.

The editor also wishes to acknowledge the assistance of his wife in seeing these materials through the press.

Nicholas Rescher
Pittsburgh
Spring, 1977

Essence and Existence

BAS C. VAN FRAASSEN

I. *Nominalism and Necessity*

THE differences between medieval nominalists and realists, which foreshadowed current philosophical disagreements, concerned existence. But the issues were not simple: realists postulated essences or real natures in order to explain the regularities in the actual world. Thus the nominalists, abhorring the existence of such abstract entities, found themselves also in a dispute over necessities: whether some things must, and others could happen, and whether these modal facts do, or are needed to, explain what actually happens.

The firm standpoint taken by the nominalists, as I understand them, was the one that became characteristic of the British empiricists later: the only necessities are those which derive from the connections among terms. As Nicholas of Autrecourt formulated it: there can be no inference from the existence or non-existence of one thing to that of another. In that case, realists held, there is no explanation to be had of the regularities in nature—they are one and all coincidences. This realist criticism was later sharply formulated by Peirce, especially in his remarks on Mill.[1]

The appearances are certainly all against the nominalists. For we do say that some things must, and others could happen, and in this way explain what does happen. Scientists, far from having a Quinean canonical idiom, speak just that way. The nominalists' first and basic move in this game is to say that all natural necessities are elliptic for conditional verbal necessities. This sheet on which I write must burn if heated, because it is paper—yes. But the only necessity that is *really* there is that all paper must burn when heated. This is so, but means only that we would not call something "paper" if it behaved differently. (This is a naive formulation, but I shall not here present the process of sophisticating it.) There are technical difficulties for logicians in making sense of this move; but when sufficiently refined, the position that all non-verbal necessities are ellipses for conditional necessities *ex vi terminorum* can be held.[2]

---

[1] C. S. Peirce, "Uniformity" in his *Essays in the Philosophy of Science*, ed. by V. Thomas (Indianapolis: Bobbs-Merrill, 1957); see especially p. 157; compare also "The Reality of Thirdness" in the same collection, especially pp. 166–167.

[2] See my "The Only Necessity is Verbal Necessity," *The Journal of Philosophy*, vol. 74 (1977), pp. 71–85.

There is however, a special problem, as Quine pointed out very early on, about necessities *de re*. In the above example, the nominalist really *denied* that this sheet must burn if heated. He replaced the necessity of the consequent by the necessity of the consequence, to use their inimitably concise jargon. What is true only, he asserted, is that this sheet *is* paper, a contingent fact, and that any paper must burn if heated, a necessary universal conditional which is not peculiarly about this sheet at all. So he denies the necessity *de re* asserted.

But we are very accustomed to assert necessities and possibilities *de re*, and are a bit suspicious of any philosophical position that accuses everyone of habitual and systematic logical error. Could we ever follow the nominalist on this issue and really feel comfortable—at home in the world of Antoine Roquentin, protagonist of *La Nausée*, who perceives every natural fact and connection as radically contingent?

In the remainder of this essay I shall examine what I believe to be the main philosophical and logical puzzles in the history of this problem.

II. *Essence and Individuation*

1. *Real possibilities*

Not just any man could hack a tree down; but Peter could. A traditional diagnosis is that each individual has an essence, which comprises at least the properties he has essentially; and for some men, though not Peter, this essence rules out hacking a tree down. Another answer, also not without historical precedent, says that some conceivable situations are really possible and others not; the conceivable situation in which Peter hacks a tree down is really possible.

What must we assume, if these two diagnoses are to agree? In the second case, it is imperative that the situation envisaged really has Peter in it, and not somebody like him. In the first case, however, a check requires only the consideration of arbitrary individuals having Peter's essence. For the two diagnoses to be the same, Peter must be the only one who has his essence: *essence individuates*.

2. *Aquinas*

This is exactly what Aquinas holds. A composite individual is one which consists of a nature received in matter. About such an individual, Aristotle had said that it is the matter which individuates

(*Metaph.*, VII, 1034d, 5–8). The essence, according to Aquinas, has to comprise both nature and matter, hence also individuates. For the essence of man is *what it is to be a man* (this includes having matter), and the essence of Socrates is *what it is to be Socrates* (which includes having this flesh and these bones; *Being and Essence* II, pp. 32–33 in Maurer tr.). For:

> That by which Socrates is man can be communicated to many; but that by which he is this man can be communicated only to one. If, therefore, Socrates were a man by that by which he is this man just as there cannot be many Socrates, so there could not be many men (*Summa Theologica*, I, q. 11, a. 3c.)

Thus essence individuates, in this case by the matter it comprises, the *thisness* over and above the *suchness*.

Before I turn to the problems with this idea, let us see how Aquinas generalizes this. Simple substances do not have a material component. Aristotle appears to rule this out (*Metaph*, VII, 8), but for Aquinas the angels are a good example. They have no matter to individuate them; so the essence can comprise only the nature. Yet the same line of reasoning applies, and Aquinas concludes that "there are as many species among them as there are individuals" (*B&E*, IV, pp. 44–45).

The soul presents a special case. We must allow for the possibility of two humans having been "specifically the same and numerically diverse," because the nature is only the *infima species* to which an individual belongs, and does not include the accidents. Yet their souls must remain distinct after death. Aquinas here has recourse to historical connection, what Reichenbach would have called *genidentity*, as a relation founded *in rem*: the two souls are individuated by *having been received* in different matter (*B&E*, V, p. 52).

I am not telling this story merely for historical interest. Individuation is a topic of interest for probability[3] and for modal logic.[4] The problem is set by subsection 1 above, because the two diagnoses of modality *de re* cannot agree unless essence individuates.

3. *Materia signata*

That Socrates *has* matter does not distinguish him from other men; only that he has *this* matter. For this reason, Aquinas introduces the distinction between matter as such and designated

---

[3] See my "Probabilities and the Problem of Individuation" in *Probabilities, Problems and Paradoxes*, ed. by S. Luckenbach (Encino, Calif.: Dickenson, 1972).

[4] Cf. D. Kaplan, "How to Russell a Frege Church," *The Journal of Philosophy*, vol. 72 (1975), pp. 716–729, which is discussed further in Section III-3 below.

matter—picture it as the distinction between water and a lake, between clay and a clod. There is an obvious reason for the introduction: matter as such does not individuate, in the following precise sense: the attribute of having matter is shared by all substances, and therefore cannot be used to single out one from another.

But Aquinas vacillates on what "signata" signifies. He speaks of place and spatial dimensions, of occupying a determinate location and volume. But surely the same observation applies again: every clod has a place and determinate spatial dimensions. So what distinguishes *this* clod is that it occupies *this* place. In other passages, Aquinas emphasizes the "this." Some commentators take "designated" to mean something like "designatable (referrable to) by us, by means of a demonstrative." However, every clod is designatable by "this"—though only *this* clod is designated by *this* use of the word "this." It seems that we are only pushing the problem back one step at each move. The individuation of substances by one of their components (say, the material component) seems only to raise the further, but parallel problem of the individuation of that component.

Some medieval writers, violating the Aristotelian relationist view of space, went so far as to introduce an individuating accident: the *ubi*, or *where-it-is-ness*, of the thing. I assume that to them the "matter" solution to the problem of individuation was so unsatisfactory that they introduced, in effect, something like absolute space. For we could not very well follow Aristotle in defining the place of a thing as constituted by the adjacent bodies, and then hold that bodies are individuated by the places they occupy.

There is a scholastic way out, and this may be why Aquinas did not seem to worry overly much about explaining "signata." The problem of individuation only arises for substances, for they alone can be subjects of predication. Socrates' matter is not a substance, and so the problem of individuation does not arise for it. That is why the invocation of designated matter does not reify the *thisness*, does not really introduce a bare particular at Socrates' core. But if it does not reify, what does it do?

It is indeed a subtle ontology which allows such gradations of identity and diversity that it can distinguish Socrates' matter from Socrates, and yet hold that the two are not distinct entities in their own right. The nominalists, already hard pressed on so many fronts, could not swallow this either. In the nominalist ontology, what is distinguishable is separable is separate. And I cannot help but agree with them. If the *thisness* is not reified in this talk of designated matter, it seems to me, we have no solution at all; but if it is so reified, the same problem will arise one step further on.

4. *Leibniz*

At the age of 17, Leibniz wrote an essay *De Principio Individui* in which he reached the bothersome conclusion that it must be the essence as a whole (not the nature or the matter alone) which individuates. Some years later, he cut the Gordian knot, after discarding prime matter altogether.

> It is not true that two substances may be exactly alike and differ only numerically, *solo numero*, and . . . what St. Thomas Aquinas says on this point regarding angels and intelligences (*quod ibi omne individuum sit species infima*) is true of all substances.
>
> (*Discourse on Metaphysics*, IX)

This is actually misleading. For Leibniz' discussion of examples shows quickly that he has not gone over to the view that the nature individuates. He has discarded prime matter, and takes the view that the accidents individuate. What it is to be Socrates comprises everything that ever happens to Socrates and indeed, everything that is true about the world which Socrates inhabits.

Any one property may be shareable; it does not follow that two individuals can have all the same properties. Leibniz asserts that they cannot. And hence, individuals are individuated by what they are like. This is a successful solution to the problem of individuation. In view of the difficulties encountered by Aquinas, this solution seems to me to be the right one. But this conclusion amounts to what Kaplan calls *anti-haecceitism*: there is no *thisness* over and above *suchness*.[5]

III. *Natures and DE RE Necessities*

1. *Leibnizian individuation and modality*

I began Part II with a pair of diagnoses of *de re* modality and asserted that these diagnoses will agree only if essence individuates. Since Leibniz discarded matter as individuating factor, and indeed any *haecceity* as opposed to *quiddity*, this would in turn require (if it is to be guaranteed) that the essence of an individual comprises all its properties.

---

[5] On this, see further below: Part III, section 3.

At this point, several mistaken inferences are commonly made. (I see these in my past self, as well as the mote in my neighbor's eye.) One conclusion is that modal distinctions (at least those made *de re*) collapse. Another is that no individual who exists in one world can be identical with one in another world ("Cross-world identification"). The two are related: Socrates' essence involves, relationally, all the facts about the world in which he lives; which facts are incompatible with the facts about any other world; no one not sharing this essence can be Socrates. But in that case, the assertion that Socrates is pug-nosed in all worlds (respectively, in all worlds in which he lives) is false (respectively, equivalent to the assertion that he is pug-nosed in this world)—where can we turn? These persuasive-sounding arguments rest on a confusion.

There are two ways in which we can construe "Socrates is pug-nosed in world α." The first is *conjunctive*: the sentence means that Socrates is pug-nosed *and* exists in α. The second is *relational*: the sentence means that a certain relation, not dissectable, holds between Socrates and α. On the first construal, "Socrates is pug-nosed" is a full-fledged statement; on the second, it is an *ellipsis* for an *indexical* sentence, namely "Socrates is pug-nosed in the actual world." The semantics of normal modal logic allow us to go on without explicitly opting for either construal, and looks as if "Socrates is pug-nosed" is being treated as a full-fledged statement. Problems are encountered with each construal as we try to make it precise.

Suppose that "Socrates is pug-nosed" is short for "Socrates is actually pug-nosed." In that case, the prefixing of a necessity operator will yield "It is necessary that Socrates is actually pug-nosed." That is like "It is, always was, and always will be true that I die on Walpurgis night, AD 2021." In other words, the modal operator has no effect at all! Since the semantics shows it does have an effect, this construal must be wrong. (But no! We could be subtle and say that "It is necessary that" turns "actually" into a bound variable, an effect which, though ever so curious, was never thought worthy of discussion.)

Suppose on the other hand that the conjunctive construal is correct. Then, *whether we opt for Leibniz or Aquinas*, Socrates cannot have different properties in different worlds! Suppose we say that Socrates could be one way in one world, and different in another world; like a man who sings in one room and silently dances a jig in another. Then we either contradict ourselves or are abandoning the conjunctive construal. For no one can sing and also be silent.

There is one further construal (which I owe to Kit Fine): "in world α" could be taken as an adverbial modification of "is pug-nosed." I believe we can classify that as a relational construal, for present purposes. And I know of no further construals.

We do not face a significant difference between haecceitists and anti-haecceitists here. Each can adopt either construal, and face the same difficulties. The conjunctive construal forces us to say that if Socrates exists in two worlds, these must be totally alike. The relational construal allows anti-haecceitists as well as haecceitists to say that Socrates exists in two worlds, being pug-nosed in one and aquiline in the other. On the conjunctive construal, I believe that only something like David Lewis' counterpart theory saves modal distinctions, and Ishiguro gave reasons to think that Leibniz toyed with such an idea.[6] The relational construal seems to me to fit much better; its difficulties cannot be insuperable given the readily applicable analogy of times and tenses. (Though it must be kept in mind that in the case of tenses we can, without reifying times, appeal to cross-time relations, an important difference.) If "It was the case in the past that" applied to a sentence in the present tense yields one in the past tense, then "It is necessary that" can surely have an equally destructive effect on the tacit "actual"—and only the lack of careful linguistic analysis at the outset was regrettable.

Let us henceforth take the relational construal for granted. With this in hand, we can make Leibniz' criteria of individuation precise. I offer two candidates:

IND–POS   No two possible entities have the same properties in all worlds.

IND–EX   No two existents in world α have all the same properties in α.

"Properties" means here occurrent properties, non-modal properties. Later on, especially in the Appendix, I shall turn to that eye-brow raising distinction, but I beg that it be accepted for now.

IND–EX implies IND–POS if we assume that each possible individual exists in at least one world. Given Leibniz' remarks about identical leaves in the garden, and being charitable about their more absurd aspects (for he was claiming much more than he should), it surely seems that he accepted the strong version IND-EX. I shall henceforth take that to be the correct one.

[6] Hidé Ishiguro, Leibniz's *Philosophy of Logic and Language* (Ithaca, N.Y.: Cornell University Press, 1972), pp. 122–125. The principle which I call IND-EX below, however, with the relational construal of properties, allows one not to go to this extreme, though the example about Sextus in the *Theodicy* indicates that Leibniz himself did.

IND–EX has a lovely consequence. Whether or not Socrates exists also in other worlds, in this world we can safely refer to him by a description that identifies him here. He is the only possible individual who actually taught Plato and was pug-nosed. It means also that at most one individual in another world can be Socrates, because Socrates cannot be both F in α and not F in α, and those two will certainly differ in some such way according to IND–EX. There is, to put it in Kaplan's jargon, no splitting or merging of transworld heir lines; in Thomason's, each individual is a substance.

2. *The distinction between nature and essence*

It may now seem that anti-haecceitism makes hardly any difference at all. What is there to it, if an anti-haecceitist can consistently say that such and such an individual in another world, though totally different from the way Socrates is here, is nevertheless Socrates? The answer is that the emphasis should lie on "consistently," which is rather a debilitating hedge. I will return to this; but first I want to explore *de re* necessities a bit further.

Terminology must receive a rude shock somewhere. Essences cannot both individuate and ground necessity. Let us call the individual's *nature* the sum total of the occurrent, qualitative properties he has necessarily. Before the Leibnizian turn, the essence and nature were distinct, but only because the essence comprised the matter as well as the nature. In other words, the properties comprised in the essence were just the properties comprised in the nature: the two senses of "accidental" non-essential and non-necessary coincided.

After the Leibnizian turn, and the above terminological choice, essence and nature are still distinct, but for very different reasons. The essence no longer comprises matter, but it now comprises all properties. "Accidental" is now vacuous except in its sense of "non-necessary," which is, "not comprised in the nature." Thus essence is still nature plus something—but the something has changed from designated matter to accidents.

The term "essence" is now often used synonymously with "nature"—hence the term "essentialism" in its current use. I would propose that we should keep some term for whatever does the individuating, and so advocate that "nature" alone be used to indicate what grounds the necessities. But it is easy to see that this does violence to my original "diagnoses" of modality *de re*: no one has ever held, to my knowledge, that the nature individuates. The two diagnoses will not coincide after the Leibnizian turn, and *that* is not a terminological matter.

This does not mean, of course, that the two sorts of mental experiments must yield different examples; only that they can. If there are sufficiently many diverse enough possible worlds, then no accident will belong to Socrates in every world in which he exists. And if that is so, a property will be comprised in Socrates' nature only if Socrates has it in every world.

Indeed, the temptation is hard to avoid now to ride roughshod over the whole scheme and say that the nature *is to be defined as* the family of properties (of the correct sort: occurrent, purely qualitative) which Socrates has in every world. And this raises the further question: do we have any serious reason to give natures a status of their own, and ask, for example, that the really possible worlds be exactly those which are logically possible and compatible with the information given when each individual's nature is specified?

I think the answer is *no*. We certainly do not have the medievals' reasons for giving such a special status to natures. Those reasons were two.

The first was that the attribution of natures would *explain* regularities in nature. Roughly: if an individual exhibits regularities in behavior, there must be a reason for that. This reason should be a necessity (a modal fact), but it should also be something *in him*; some real component or aspect of him that explains why he must act this way.

Perhaps our puzzlement can be allayed a little if we phrase it very anachronistically. Suppose that we *describe* a regularity in Socrates' behavior by saying that he is F, and *explain* it by saying that he is F in every world. Now the description shows a relation between Socrates and something real (say, his environment), while the explanation adds to this his relations to things which are unreal (other possible worlds). Nothing that is real can be explained by relations to things which are not real. (Not my view! But let us continue.) Therefore the modal statement can at most be an intermediate step in the explanation. And that is fine if it in turn follows from the fact that Socrates has a real nature which is thus or so. For that nature he has already in this world, *in toto*, and so the final appeal in the explanation is to a reality.

I do not find this sort of consideration reason enough to posit natures as independent elements in the scheme of things; but then, I have different views on explanation.

The second reason may sound even more *outré* to modern ears. The Aristotelian–Thomist tradition seemed to harbour the conviction that all necessities about the world are somehow grounded in individuals. That is, the natures of the individuals determine how they develop if isolated, and how they react if interfered with. From this, the whole story of the universe follows, to the extent that it is deterministic.

That view is implausible in the light of the form which postulates of modern science take. As a simple example, take conservation of matter: this does not say of any individual that it cannot increase or decrease in quantity; but it says of all individuals that they cannot *jointly* increase or decrease in quantity.

The correct conclusion, in my opinion, is that we should not pay too much attention to natures and essences; they form a picture that no longer guides our modal reasoning, though once it did. The possible world picture is a genuine modern innovation, in keeping with modern times. We can reconstruct the idea of a nature to some extent—for example, as the sum total of (occurrent, qualitative) properties which the individual has necessarily. But the reconstruction can never play the role for us that its original enjoyed.

3. *Kaplan*

David Kaplan recently wrote on some of these issues, describing Russell and himself as haecceitists, Frege and Church as anti-haecceitists.[7] As far as the implications of the positions are concerned, my conclusions so far will be seen to agree with his, after I draw a few more connections.

Anti-haecceitism does not make it inconsistent to say that the man called Callias in world W is identical with (or distinct from) the man called Socrates here. It does, however, remove the basis for such assertions. If the anti-haecceitist is right, and the *infima species* to which Socrates and Callias belonged in life are the same, then God has no objective basis for judging *this* soul by Socrates' actions and *that* one by Callias'. The differences between them were all acquired after death (assuming the simultaneous death of Socrates and Callias, and thinking it not so different in relation to the hereafter from the birth of identical twins here). Yet God has two souls before him, and wishes to judge both Callias and Socrates; there can be no injustice in whatever choice he makes in the designation—for there are no relevant differences between them. The point is, though, that his choice will be conventional. (I am not sure that transworld retributive justice is really consistent with such a view!) Does this not contradict my previous conclusion that we can consistently say: *that* one is Socrates and *this* one is not? For should

[7] See footnote 4 above.

that not imply that we can, still consistently, add: hence God is wrong? But God would be wrong only if the contrary assertion (which he made) is somehow ruled out. To say that we can consistently add one assertion or the other, does not mean that one of the two is somehow really true all along! Only that we can consistently say that it was true all along!

Let me argue the case somewhat differently too. We describe one situation, and then we again describe a situation, and see if they are really different. The first is: this soul is Socrates, that one Callias. The second is: that soul is Socrates, the first one Callias. Now we ask whether there are any facts which differentiate the two described situations. The anti-haecceitist answers *no*. By the identity of indiscernibles we assert that there is really only one situation; what is objectively true is what is common to the two descriptions. Any remainder is 'conventional'. The case is quite analogous to Max Black's universe consisting of two equal black spheres. Counterfactual properties may differentiate these; but if the objective basis for such counterfactuals is denied, and the identity of indiscernibles upheld, it follows that there is no such world—the nearest to answering the description contains only a single sphere.[8]

Won't this make difficulties for modal logic? In a model structure, we could surely have two worlds, totally alike, except in that in the one, it is Socrates who is denied heaven, and in the other, Callias. Should we rule out such a model structure, on the basis that it has one world twice over?

Not at all. So much in model logic semantics is fictional that a little duplication in possible worlds, for the sake of faithfully representing certain patterns of inference in our language, will not hurt. We just say then that possible worlds which are isomorphic in a certain sense 'represent the same possible reality'.[9]

Although the conventionality of identifications *pace* anti-haecceitists may need to introduce only a limited amount of fictionalism into the analysis of modalities, I think that the following remarks by David Wiggins will apply in substance:

> Surely possible worlds are not really things we find or discover. Rather we make them. . . . So *if* we see possible worlds as the right way to decide (4) [Note: (4) was the formula $(\forall x)(\forall y)[(x = y) \supset \Box(y = x)]$], I conclude that a postulational or constructional view of them may provide a sounder framework than the realist one. Within this framework there will

---

[8] Cf. my *Introduction to the Philosophy of Time and Space* (New York: Random House, 1970), pp. 63–65.

[9] Cf. Kaplan, p. 727.

be no more problem about identifying the individuals in a possible world . . . than there ever is for one to know what named individuals one is thinking about.[10]

If we make, create possible worlds, like we make models, than we can make several which correspond to the same possible reality, going beyond its facts in alternative, arbitrary ways.

One warning is in order. If modal logic is extended to deal with probability, the truth of a statement may hinge on how many worlds there are in a certain proposition. As with all technical matters, however, you can always have your cake or eat it by one dodge or another; in this case by counting either individual worlds or isomorphism classes thereof, depending on what probability assessment type you consider correct.[11]

A quick look will verify that now, after having viewed the Identity of Indiscernibles at work "one level up" as it were, we are in agreement with Kaplan's statement of the issues. He does say that anti-haecceitism "holds that for entities of distinct possible worlds there is no notion of trans-world being" but he explains this as not ruling out such identifications in thought:

> Our interests may cause us to *identify* individuals of distinct worlds, but we are then creating something—a trans-world continuant—of a kind different from anything given by the metaphysics. Although the Anti-Haecceitist may seem to assert that no possible individual exists in more than one possible world, that view is properly reserved for the Haecceitist who holds to an unusually rigid brand of metaphysical determinism. (p. 723.)

Kaplan also carefully distinguishes this issue from that of *Actualism* versus *Possibilism*. The former holds that there are no (exist no) possible individuals which are not actual. I suppose one would expect an Actualist to develop only modal logics in which all quantifiers range over actual existents. But here again there are technical dodges; the Actualist may *reconstruct* the phrase "for all possible individuals x" in some way that makes philosophical sense to him (and hence does not involve commitment to the reality of possibles) and has the formal structure of a quantifier too.[12]

[10] His "The DE RE 'must'; A Note on the Logical Form of Essentialist Claims," in *Truth and Meaning, Essays in Semantics*, ed. by G. Evans and J. K. McDowell (Oxford, 1976); with an appendix by C. A. B. Peacocke.

[11] This is what Carnap did in effect with his measures m^+ and m^*; see my "Probabilities and Problem of Individuation," footnote 3 above.

[12] As Lambert and I have done, showing that the utilization of the usual form of semantics carries no ontic commitment in this area: see our "Meaning Relations, Possible Objects, and Possible Worlds," in *Philosophical Problems in Logic*, ed. by K. Lambert (Dordrecht: Reidel, 1970), pp.1–19.

There is one point on which I disagree with Kaplan—but I think his view on this point is tentative. He writes:

> If one regards the usual form of quantification into modal and other intensional contexts—modality *de re*—as legitimate (without special explanations), then again one seems committed to some form of Haecceitism. (P. 725.)

The crucial phrase may be "without special explanations." For when Kaplan has allowed *conventional* transworld identifications to the anti-haecceitist, he has certainly allowed him the power to make special necessary *de re* statements true. Suppose for example that our interests cause us to identify—to use his phrase—Socrates in every possible word, and in each case we select an individual with a pug nose. (It may be a necessary *de dicto* fact that there is some pugnosed individual, in which case this may happen.) Then "Socrates is necessarily pugnosed" will be true, and indeed, so will "Socrates necessarily exists." If conventional identifications are allowed, their influence will extend throughout the language.

The Anti-Haecceitist will certainly have a low view of *de re* necessities, because for him they can be true only given those conventional identifications. But as in so many areas, it may be insisted that this is a convenient fiction to save the phenomena of inference patterns in our language. *Our inferential reasoning is guided by a picture, the picture that bewitches us—and that is the picture of extreme metaphysical realism.* Hence the logical theorist must draw on that picture to fashion his semantic models.

IV. *Modal Logic*

1. *A sketch of a nominalist position*

The preceding discussion has given the picture of a paradigm nominalist, as I see him: he is an anti-haecceitist, follows Leibniz on identity and individuation, and believes that any necessities there are, derive from relations among terms (verbal or logical necessities). Perhaps if there were natures (real dispositional or causal properties, propensities) there would be necessary connections in nature— but there are not. How does he make sense of the way we talk and reason?

Let me first tell his story simply, naively, as it would sound before logical difficulties force him to grow *raffiné*. The story has two parts.

At bottom, everything that can be said about the world, can be said in purely general statements, without modalities. There is no

thisness beyond *suchness*, but every actual individual is individuated already by the properties it has in this world; hence can be
denoted in principle by a definite description (in which the quantifier ranges over actual existents alone). At this bottom level the
only necessity we can countenance is purely logical or verbal
necessity which, like God, is no respecter of persons. In this
modality, whatever Peter can do, Paul can do also. A semantic
representation of this will use a conventional identification of
individuals in different worlds, but since every individual plays each
possible role in some possible world, *every* choice of conventional
identifications (which does not violate IND–EX) yields the same
result.

To make sense of our world in a *convenient* fashion, however, we
raise certain regularities to the status of laws and (not indepen-
dently!) certain attributes to the status of natures. In the formal
mode, this means that some statements assume the office of assumptions which may be tacitly used in all reasoning, and certain predicates are chosen to form a classificatory scheme. Once this is done,
we produce relative (or, tacitly conditional) modal qualifiers.

Let me give an example of how classificatory predicates enter into
modality. "Human" and "British" do (in certain contexts) play this
classificatory role, while "dolly-bird" does not. As a result, I can tell
the distinguished philosopher that she could be a dolly-bird if she
liked, but I cannot tell myself that I could be British—at least, not as
Britons understand it. Of course, what regularities in nature we
believe there to be, influence at once which predicates we use as
classificatory, and which statements we allow as tacit assumptions—
the two sources for the "impure" or "common" use of "could."

When we look at iterated uses of modal qualifiers, we perceive
that these distinctions are reified. In the semantic interpretation,
each world is equipped with its own division of regularities into
coincidences and laws, and the conventional identification of individuals across worlds has to respect the classificatory attributes
(Socrates has, in every world with at least our laws, at least those
properties which here belong to his nature). The result of this
reification is that, although we cannot imagine a physical law
violated except when the corresponding regularity is broken, we can
talk as if this is possible. That is, after the reification we do not rule
out that this world could have exactly the same history but different
laws—by coincidence in the part which the laws leave
indeterministic.

Our language and reasoning is guided by a picture, a picture which bewitches us, the picture described by extreme realism.

2. *The difficulties with the sketched position*

According to this nominalist then, pure logical necessity is no respecter of persons; physical necessities and necessities *de re* are impurities produced by our theorizing activity. They are produced when we start using ellipses; the information that certain regularities are to be assumed and certain properties to be used as classificatory, is left tacit.

The difficulties are these. If physical necessity is just logical necessity relative to certain assumptions (implication by laws) then there should be a translation schema of form

$$(1) \qquad\qquad \boxdot A \equiv \Box(P \supset A)$$

However, since the pure necessity $\Box$ is of S5 type, any relative necessity $\boxdot$ related to it by 1 is also of S5 type. Secondly, it does not seem that you can produce necessities *de re* this way unless you had some already. Given 1, the statement

$$(2) \qquad\qquad (\exists y)(\exists x)(\boxdot Ax \,\&\, \sim\boxdot Ay)$$

will be true only if for some other statement B,

$$(3) \qquad\qquad (\exists y)(\exists x)(\Box Bx \,\&\, \sim\Box By)$$

is true. Some statements of form $(\exists y)\Box A$ are perhaps harmless because they follow from $(\forall y)\Box A$ which in turn follows from $\Box(\forall y)A$. But 3 cannot very well be of that harmless sort, for if we replace the existential quantifiers in 3 by universal ones, we get a contradiction.

The first problem shows, if the nominalist wants to hold his position for relative necessities in general, that 1 is incorrect. Whatever is to be meant by the idea that what is physically necessary is what the physical laws imply, it cannot be explicated that way. This problem I have discussed in an earlier paper, and I believe that an adequate explication is available,[13] The second problem concerns the correct understanding of what modality *de re* is, logically or semantically. For this problem is a problem only if we believe that an assertion of form 3 must be an assertion of necessity *de re*. Intuitively we also feel that such an assertion must be

---

[13] See footnote 2.

peculiarly about some individual. Yet in ordinary quantified S5 we can derive

(4) $(\exists x)(\exists y)(\Box(Bx \;\&\; \sim\!By \cdot \supset Bx) \;\&\; \sim\!\Box(Bx \;\&\; \sim\!By \cdot \supset By))$

from the premise

(5) $\qquad\qquad (\forall)(\forall y) \sim \Box(Bx \;\&\; \sim\!By \cdot \supset By)$

which seems to give no information that is peculiarly about one thing more than another. The correct understanding of what makes an assertion of necessity *de re* was developed in successive papers by a number of writers (Terry Parsons, Pavel Tichy, Jonathan Broido, Allen Hazen, Kit Fine, a.o.) and I shall draw on their work to continue the story.

3. *Purity*

At the time A. N. Prior was discussing this, the distinction drawn between sentences which are modal de re and those modal *de dicto* was indeed identified with the syntactic distinction: quantifiers do, or do not, reach into the scope of modal operators. But this syntactic distinction cannot correspond to any semantic distinction, *because it is not invariant under logical equivalence.* For example, $(\forall x)\Box(Fx \vee \sim\!Fx)$, being a tautology, is logically equivalent to $\Box(\forall x)Fx \vee \sim\!Fx)$, when $\Box$ is the pure logical necessity (truth in *all* possible worlds).[14]

To explain briefly: let us call a *permutation* of a possible world an operation that turns it into another possible world in which the numbers of individuals having given (occurrent) properties are the same. For example, let w_1 have individuals a and b, and suppose that this is totally described by saying that a is F in w_1 and b is not F in w_1. Then a permutation will produce world w_2, in which b but not a is F. We consider a model in which each world has the same inhabitants, and our quantifier ranges over them. Then a sentence is *de dicto*, informally characterized, if its truth value remains the same under such permutations.[15] For example, $(\exists x)Fx$ which is true in w_1 is also true in w_2; $(\exists x)\sim\!\Box Fx$ is also like that, even though a quantifier reaches into the scope of a modal operator.

---

[14] I do not know who first made that crucial observation (hindsight shows it implicit in early discussions), but I saw it first explicitly formulated in a paper by Pavel Tichy. And Tichy also supplied the semantic distinction, for the special case of quantificational S5, and which is made in a generalized form in the recent papers of Kit Fine.

[15] The criterion I give here is not the same as Tichy's. It is formulated in the same terms and I have proved some relations among the two that indicate they can be put to the same use. See Appendix.

Suppose now that we are considering a second property G, that a and b are both G in w_1 and in w_2. But the model contains besides these worlds exactly one other one, namely w_3 in which a and b are both F and a is G, but b is not G.

	F	$\sim F$	G	$\sim G$
w_1	a	b	a, b	
w_2	b	a	a, b	
w_3	a, b		a	b

The permutation of a and b still leads us from w_1 to w_2. But in w_1 the sentence $(\exists x)(Fx \ \& \ \Box Gx)$ is true, while in w_2 it is false. So this sentence, by the criterion I have given, is modal *de re*. And indeed, it is true in w_1 because the thing which is F there—namely a—is the one which is necessarily G. The statement $Fa \ \& \ \Box Ga$ is *really* about a; unlike, say, $\Diamond Ga$ which reports a fact that is equally true about b.

This suggests a criterion of *aboutness*: proposition P is *peculiarly about a* only if, for some individual b, the permutation which exchanges a and b but leaves all other individuals the same, leads from a world in which P has one truth-value to a world in which P has the opposite value. Such a statement would be *singular* in a real (not just syntactic) sense. The phenomenon of modality *de re* derives from modal singular statements, after a simple generalization.

Two remarks are in order about the above characterizations. The diagram I used will show at once that in simple cases, the ideas are the same as the ones Carnap used for probability: "state-descriptions" gotten from each other by permutations of individual constants belong to the same "structure-description." This syntactic way of looking at it will do for all finite cases.

Now in syntax, we have a distinction between atomic predicates and others. That has no semantic basis. But without it, how could I define a permutation of worlds? Some properties, modal ones, do not keep the same number of instances as we move from world w_1 to its permutation w_2. Well, what happens in the description of the model is that a certain family of properties must be singled out as *significant*; they alone are used to define permutation. Logically, they can be any family; but when we interpret a language by them (giving one to each atomic predicate), we may prefer to exercise some care so that sentences in which modal qualifiers do not appear, are not modal *de re*.

It may also be noticed from the diagram that the *de re* phenomenon disappears if we add a fourth world, the result of permuting *a* and *b* in w_3. Call a model *full* if for each world it contains, it also has in it all permutations thereof. In such a model, we may still distinguish singular from general propositions, but the phenomenon of *de re* modality disappears. Perhaps not only nominalists will agree that to represent pure logical or verbal necessity, only full models are appropriate.

There is still the anti-haecceitist claim that only general propositions are significant. We may identify general propositions now as ones not being peculiarly about anything (nor peculiarly about any special set of things, if you like, by a simple extension of the notion). So these are propositions which are such that, if they are true in *w* they are also true in all permutations of *w*. We have just remarked that in a full model, with the necessity interpreted in its widest sense (truth in all worlds), this claim will not rule out modalizing—not even quantifying into modal contexts. Nor does it raise difficulties for conjunction, negation, other extensional connectives. What this means is that if you start with general propositions in a full model, and combine them in the usual ways, you will always have only general propositions.

But still, there *are* others; for example, the proposition which is true in exactly world w_1, nowhere else, or the one which is true in exactly those worlds in which *a* exists. The interpretation of language in this model will have to proceed by a selection, not only of significant properties (candidates for being intensions of our predicates), but also of significant propositions (candidates for being what sentences say). This is not as novel a procedure as it may seem. Quite apart from its recurrent appearance in recent studies in modal logic, it was used in quantum logic from the beginning.

4. *Impurities*

In this world there is an individual with a pugnose, and so there is in that other world. We may say that these two individuals are the same. The decision to do so is, after all, only a decision about how we construct a semantic representation, for nowhere else are possible worlds to be found.

The identification may have to be limited in some ways. If the classificatory scheme we adopt is to play a reason-guiding role, then identifications should follow classifications. Perhaps Linnaeus would say that to him, a geranium with twenty-four petal flowers is inconceivable; perhaps, since biologists now use the phylogenetic classification, we should say that a geranium descended from a sweet-pea is impossible: whatever its observable characteristics, it would *ipso facto* not be a geranium. If this is so, the classificatory properties—the natural kinds—will have this modal status:

(1) $$Qx \supset \Box Qx$$

For any world counted as possible relative to this one, will have Socrates identified as an individual which has just those properties which place Socrates in his natural kind here—and so on.

From 1 and the information that Socrates really does have property Q, we deduce that he has Q necessarily. This conclusion can be a singular proposition: exchanging Socrates and Babylon will change its truth-value. But how does the anti-haecceitist get singular propositions in the first place? We might guess that if $\Box Qx$ *were* explicated as $\Box(P \supset Qx)$, then we would get no singular propositions at all unless P were singular. Since in the preceding section, we found the anti-haecceitist limiting himself to a family of general propositions, we wonder where he gets P in that case.

But the guess is wrong. For IND–EX guarantees that Socrates can be identified by definite description in each world in which he exists, without letting the variables inside the description range outside that world. Suppose that Socrates = (the x)(Rx), we can give the information that Socrates has Q with (physical) necessity by

(2) $$(\exists y)(y = (\text{the } x)(Rx) \ \& \ \Box Qy)$$

Is this then a general proposition? Well, the appearances do not speak against it. However, it is difficult to say more, because in what I consider the correct explication, $\Box Qy$ turns out to be an indexical, i.e., *context-dependent* statement.

I shall have to leave the matter here for now. The question whether the full treatment will not also impart something indexical to the name "Socrates"—since after all, in some other world, Socrates is probably not identical with (the x)(Rx)—is a challenging one, and not one I can answer at present.

This ends the discussion, except for the Appendix which elaborates some of the logical points, and a general remark about philosophy of logic. The phenomena, for us, are patterns of assertion and inference. This means that we do not have the task of representing the way the world is, but only the way it is thought of: the picture that guides reasoning. If this point is ignored, then we find ourselves doing a particularly naive sort of pre-Kantian metaphysics, trying to correlate all aspects of our models to reality.

In that case, to give an example, we would have to face the question: what difference in status is there between the facts reported in that tacit antecedent P of assertions of physical necessity, and ordinary facts? In other words, we would have to discover an objective distinction between law-like and accidental regularities. In my opinion, there is no such distinction, except in so far as we create it for ourselves. On this point, logic should be firmly neutral, of course. What we should hold only is that we can save the common phenomena of inference, if we regard the agents as thinking of the world as surrounded by a halo of alternative possible worlds, actuality but an arbitrary fragment of an intricately woven web of possibilities—the attributes decreed to be divided, each after its kind, and the regularities also, each after its kind. If *this* is the picture that bewitches us, then *that* is the way we reason.

APPENDIX: FULL MODELS

The nominalist picture of the world can be reified as a full model, with only general propositions classed as significant. I base this assertion on Autrecourt's dictum that the existence or non-existence of one thing cannot be inferred from that of another (which, his discussion of causality indicates, should apply to events at different times), and my conviction that Leibniz' principle of the identity of indiscernibles in the form IND–EX, is the logical continuation of the nominalist critique of medieval realism. This Appendix will describe such models, and relate them to recent work in modal logic; but I shall restrict myself to simple cases and results. For a truly comprehensive treatment, with new and exciting results, the reader is referred to recent papers of Kit Fine.[16]

1. *The invariance of DE DICTO formulas*

Pavel Tichy made a proposal concerning the semantic correlate of the notion of *de re* necessity, for the logic Q1S5 which is semantically the simplest quantified modal logic.[17] The simplicity derives from the assumption that there is a single domain D of entities, which all exist in every possible world. We assume the usual syntax: &, ~, □.

[16] Kit Fine, "Properties, Propositions, and Sets" *Journal of Philosophical Logic*, 6 (1977).

[17] Pavel Tichy, "On DE DICTO Modalities in Quantified S5," *Journal of Philosophical Logic*, vol. 2 (1973), pp. 387–392.

A *world* on D is a map w of all n-ary predicates into D^n, for every integer n. A *model structure* Σ on D is a set of worlds on D. A permutation of D is a one-to-one map of D onto D. If g is such a permutation, define

(a) $g(w)(P^n) = g(w(P^n))$—call $g(w)$ a permutation of w.
(b) $g(\Sigma) = \{g(w): w \in \Sigma\}$
(c) Σ^1 is a p-*variant* of Σ if there is a one-to-one map F of Σ^1 onto Σ such that $F(w)$ is some permutation of w.

It will be understood that if $X \subseteq D^n$, then $g(X)$ is the set of n-tuples $\langle g(x_1), \ldots, g(x_n) \rangle$ such that $\langle x_1, \ldots, x_n \rangle$ is in X. Note that p-variants of Σ are easily produced: you replace each world in Σ by one or more permutations thereof. So $g(\Sigma)$ is one p-variant of Σ, of a very simple kind. I add one more notion, which Tichy did not need:

(d) Σ is a *full model structure* exactly if $\Sigma^0 \subseteq \Sigma$, where $\Sigma^0 = \bigcup\{g(\Sigma): g \text{ a permutation of } D\}$

All p-variants of Σ are parts of it when Σ is full; Σ^0 is the largest p-variant of Σ.

Let α be an assignment of values in D to all variables. Then $g(\alpha)$ will be another such assignment defined by $g(\alpha)(x) = g(\alpha(x))$. If Σ^1 and Σ are as described in (c) above, let g_w be the permutation such that $w = g_w(F(w))$, for each w in Σ^1.

Tichy proved, for sentences A (which may have free variables):

Lemma For all α, α satisfies A at $F(w)$ in Σ iff $g_w(\alpha)$ satisfies A at w in Σ^1, when no variable is free in any subformula of A which has the form $\Box B$.

This looks a bit complicated, but it can be stated succinctly with a bit of jargon. The lemma has form "ϕ, when ψ." If ϕ is always the case, let us call A **p-immune*. If ψ is the case, call A *syntactic de dicto*. Then the lemma says:

All *syntactic de dicto* formulas are **p-immune*.

Formulas like $(\exists x)\Box Fx$ are not generally **p-immune. So Tichy's proposal is this: let us **p-immunity as the semantic correlate of the intuitive notion of being *de dicto*. We cannot get the syntactic and semantic notions to coincide, because the syntactic property is not invariant under logical equivalence. But that just means that the syntactic explication was a bad one.

I will now propose a different semantic characterization of *de dicto*, using full models. The idea is that if entity a has property F

necessarily in Σ, and this F is not something that everything must have, then the addition of some permutations of worlds to Σ will destroy this necessity. The happy outcome is that my proposal and Tichy's turn out to agree exactly; this is evidence that they are good.

Definition. A is *-*invariant* in Σ exactly if for all w in Σ^0, and all g and α, $g(\alpha)$ satisfies A at $g(w)$ in Σ^0 iff and only if α satisfies A at w in Σ.

Lemma 1. If A is *p-immune, then A is *-invariant.

Σ^0 is a p-variant of Σ by the map $F(w)$ defined by: if $w = g(w^1)$ then $F(w) = w^1$, and $g_w = g$. So if A is p-immune, then we conclude that α satisfies A at $F(w)$ in Σ exactly if g_w (α) satisfies A at w in Σ^0. Supposing now that w in Σ^0 equals $g(w^1)$, w^1 in Σ, then this becomes: α satisfies A at w^1 in Σ exactly if g (α) satisfies A at g (w^1) in Σ^0. But when this is always true, A is *-invariant by definition.

Lemma 2. If Σ_1 is a p-variant of Σ, then $\Sigma_1^0 = \Sigma^0$

This is very simple to prove because (a) permutations are again permutations, and (b) every permutation has an inverse.

Theorem. A is *p-immune exactly if it is *-invariant. Half of this was proved in Lemma 1; suppose then that A is *-invariant. Let Σ be a model structure and Σ_1 a p-variant thereof, by map F of Σ_1 onto Σ, and $g_w(F(w)) = w$ as before.

Suppose now that A is not *p-immune, and that Σ_1 shows this: say α satisfies A at $F(w)$ in Σ but g_w (α) does not satisfy A at w in Σ_1. (This is general enough, for then the opposite case occurs with $\sim A$.) For simplicity, let $w^1 = F(w)$, $w = g(w^1)$. Then

  (i) α satisfies A at w^1 in Σ
  (ii) $g(\alpha)$ does not satisfy A at $g(w^1)$ in Σ_1

Assuming now that A is *-invariant, we deduce from (i) and (ii) the following corollaries:

  (ii) g (α) satisfies A at $g(w^1)$ in Σ^0
  (iij) g (α) satisfies $\sim A$ at $g(w^1)$ in Σ_1^0

Here (iij) follows because we can use the identity permutation which leaves everything alone. The second lemma shows that these two corollaries contradict each other, which proves the theorem.

2. *Singular and General Propositions*

In the preceding section, we were concerned with language, and that may obscure distinctions which need attention. The primitive predicates are not meant to have any special status, yet the properties they express may play a special role. Specifically, we said that a world *is* a map of primitive predicates into sets of n-tuples of elements of the domain ($w(P)$ is the *extension* of P in w). As a result, the extension of such a predicate P will have the same size in any permutation of world w as in w itself. This is not true of extensions of predicates generally. In section IV-2 I drew a table depicting a system of three worlds. If in those worlds, we ask for the extensions of predicate $W = (F- \& \Box G-)$ we find that it has instances in world w_1 but not in w_2, although w_2 is formed by a permutation from w_1.

This suggests that the request for full models is not so much a requirement on the possible world structure as on how the language is interpreted: atomic predicates should only get a certain sort of property to express.

The principle IND–EX can also be given content only if we start with a division of properties. I suppose we could take it to mean: for each interpretation of the language and each entity e and each world w, there must be a predicate ψ in the language, formed without using modal terms, such that e is the only thing in the extension of ψ in w. But it is hard to believe that Leibniz could require this of the language we actually speak, which could so easily be a fragment of a larger one that we could speak. If on the other hand, we can just make up any property by pasting extensions together, then e will always be the only thing that has Z in w, where we *define* Z to have extension $\{e\}$ in each world. That deprives the principle of content.

Of course, Leibniz must have had in mind properties with a certain status, having to do with what we can observe, in our own world. This is not anathema to nominalism; everyone agrees that we can readily observe whether or not Socrates is among the pugnosed, and not whether he is possibly aquiline. To give content to our distinctions without a detour through language we must therefore single out a family of significant properties.

In model structure Σ a proposition is any set of worlds. A monadic property is any map of the domain D into propositions; we say that P is true in w if $w \in P$ and that e has G in w if $G(e)$ is true in w. Similarly, an n-adic property is a map of D^n into the propositions. A model will be equipped with a set of worlds, a domain, a family of properties.

A *model* is a triple $\Sigma = \langle W, D, F \rangle$ where W and D are non-empty sets, and F a family of properties (of various degrees). Let us call the *complexion* of F the map $\| : F \times W \to \bigcup_{n=1}^{\infty} P(D^n)$ such that $|G, w| = \{z : w \in G(z)\}$, which assigns to each property G in F and world w

the extension of G in w. Call $|-, w|$ the complexion of F in w. Then a *full model* is one such that

(a) the complexion of F in w uniquely determines w
(b) if g is a permutation of D, and w a world, then there is also in W a world $g(w)$ where F has the complexion resulting from the effect of g on the complexion of F in w. (By (a), this $g(w)$ is unique.)
(c) if e, e^1 are individuals in D, w is in W, then there is a property G in F such that one of e, e^1 belongs to $|G, w|$ and the other does not.

Clause (c) build in IND–EX. What operations on D are permutations of worlds, corresponding to permutations of individuals, is determined by what is in F.

A proposition P is *peculiarly about* individual e if we can change the truth value of P by permuting e with another individual e^1 (while leaving all other individuals fixed), but cannot change that truth-value by any permutation which leaves e fixed. For example, let P be the set of worlds in which Socrates is pug-nosed, and suppose that not everyone is pug-nosed in all those worlds. In that case take some individual, say Callias, who is not pug-nosed, and permute the two. This means that w was in $P = Pug$ (Socrates) and not in Pug (Callias), but that permutation $g(w)$ is in Pug (Callias), not in Pug (Socrates). Hence the truth-value was changed. If the model is not full, we should test by p-variants of the whole model structure.

Other propositions may be more immune to such operations, refusing to change their truth-value unless many entities are permuted, not just two. A *completely* general proposition is one that is immune to all permutations. We note that in a full model, no proposition peculiarly about a particular entity (let us call such propositions *singular*) can be necessary, for the necessary proposition is there closed under all permutations.

Is the contrary true? Are all completely general propositions necessary? Not at all. Call w and w^1 *isomorphic* if $w^1 = g(w)$ for some permutation g. There can certainly be non-isomorphic worlds in a full model. But if P is the set of worlds isomorphic to w, or the union of a family of such isomorphism classes, then P is completely general. The set of worlds in which "There are seventeen houses" is true is thus. It is therefore not immediately absurd to say, for example, that all of science, or of our knowledge, or of what we can discover about the world in which we live, consists in general propositions.

Indeed, we can hold that a language could be so constituted that its sentences express only completely general propositions, as long as the connectives in this language correspond to sufficiently pure, "logical" operations. These operations are:

(a) generalized Boolean: $-P = W - P$;

$$\cap \phi = \{x \in W: x \in P \text{ for all } P \text{ in } \phi\}$$

(b) pure necessity $\quad \Box P = \begin{cases} W \text{ if } P = W \\ \Lambda \text{ otherwise} \end{cases}$

This includes quantification. For let A be a formula in a language, α an assignment of values in D to the variables. Then the proposition expressed by A relative to α is $A(\alpha) = \{w: \alpha \text{ satisfies } A \text{ in } w\}$. The sentence $(\forall x)A$ then expressed, relative to α,

$$(\forall x)A(\alpha) = \cap \{A(\alpha^1): \alpha^1 =_x \alpha\}$$

so this is a special case of generalized Boolean meet.

That these operations preserve, in a full model, the quality of being impervious to permutations, is clear. We might even call *that* the distinguishing mark of a pure, "logical" operation.[18]

University of Toronto
and
University of Southern California

[18] The research for this paper was supported by a Canada Council grant. I wish to thank Hidé Ishiguro, David Kaplan, Karel Lambert, and David Wiggins for much helpful correspondence and discussion.

On Existence, Tense, and Logical Form

R. M. MARTIN

WHATEVER may be the true nature of things and of the conceptions which we have of them . . . , in the operations of reasoning they are dealt with as a number of separate entities or *units*," the English mathematician A. B. Kempe noted in 1885 in his "Memoir on the Theory of Mathematical Form," a neglected work much admired by Peirce, Royce, Whitehead, and Woodger, among others[1]. "These units come under consideration under a variety of garbs—as material objects," Kempe continues, "intervals or periods of time, processes of thought, points, lines, statements, relationships, arrangements, algebraical expressions, operators, operations, etc., etc.—occupy various positions, and are otherwise variously circumstanced. . . . The units which we have to consider exhibit endless variety; thus we may have a material object dealt with as one unit, a quality it possesses as another, a statement about it as a third, and a position it occupies in space as a fourth. The task of specifying the units which are considered in an investigation may in some cases be one of considerable difficulty, and mistakes are likely to occur unless the operation is conducted with great care."[2]

How modern this admirable passage is. Kempe's "units" are the individuals constituting the universe of discourse or ontology of a given system. They may, of course, be subdivided into many kinds, and note how catholic the list is—material objects, times, mental processes, mathematical objects, linguistic objects, relationships, qualities, positions, circumstances. Whatever "the true nature of things" is, Kempe notes, these various kinds of entities presumably must be regarded as units so far as concerns "the operations of [our] reasoning." As philosophers we should be concerned surely with both the true nature of things, with the operations of our reasoning, and, above all perhaps, with the operations of our reasoning concerning the units that make up the true nature of things. Nothing less than a reasonably full account of this latter will satisfy a

---

[1] *Philosophical Transactions of the Royal Society*, vol. 177 (1886); pp. 1–70.
[2] *Ibid.*

logicometaphyscian worth his salt.[3] To give such an account of existence and logic is the task before us.

In following the new way of words in its most sophisticated form, but not neglecting the old way of things, we should assay first an account of the logical structure of the sentences employed to state our metaphysical view. And this has turned out of course to be enormously difficult. To succeed, no less than the whole totality of sentences needed must be subjected to exact logical analysis and logical forms or linguistic structures for them supplied. The variety of kinds of sentences needed, even just declarative ones, is very great, and logicians to date have been concerned with only a few of them of quite simple structure. A considerable expansion of the usual logic (first-order quantification theory with non-logical predicates) must take place before we can gain a suitable instrument for linguistic and metaphysical analysis.[4]

The metaphysical form of a sentence should be distinguished from its deep structure or linguistic form. To give the latter, in principle, for all sentences, and to formulate the full theory concerning them, is, roughly, the task of structural linguistics. But this science is not concerned, at least not primarily or especially, with "the true nature of things." The structural linguist will do his job pretty much the same whatever metaphysical view he might be sympathetic to—should he happen to be sympathetic to any. Once the structural linguist has provided a form, the logico-metaphysician will wish to go a step further and study how that form may be made to harmonize with his conception of, and ways of talking about, the true nature of things. Whatever these latter may be, "existence" will still be allowed to apply to the individuals or units arrived at at the earlier stage of analysis. They may not constitute the "really real," or the fundamental ground of all being, but still they should be allowed to exist, it would seem, in the way in which we ordinarily use that word. The metaphysician should not be allowed to flaunt ordinary usage in this respect.

To gain a system of sufficient breadth to provide logical forms for a very extensive set of sentences of natural language, let us proceed as follows. To the ordinary quantification theory with non-logical predicates, let us add the calculus of individuals (essentially

---

[3] For more along similar lines, see the author's *Logic, Language, and Metaphysics* (New York University Press, New York: 1971) and "On Peirce, Bradley, and the Doctrine of Continuous Relations," *Idealistic Studies*, to appear.

[4] See especially the author's *Events, Reference, and Logical Form* (The Catholic University of America Press, Washington: to appear).

Lésniewski's mereology). And to this let us add the theory of virtual classes and relations, which is merely quantificational theory in a kind of notational disguise.[5] Even so, the new notations are useful. With just this much we have a considerable bit of theory in which several different kinds of expressions for existence can be defined.

First of course there is the existential quantifier. A sentence of the form '$(Ex)Fx$' where F is a virtual class, expresses that at least one object or "unit" of the universe of discourse of the language is a member of F. Although '(Ex)' is commonly called an *existential* quantifier, it is existential only by proxy, being concerned only with the units of the universe of discourse howsoever taken, and not necessarily with the real nature of things. Then there is the '$E!$', of *Principia Mathematica,* *14, for descriptional existence, where '$E!(\iota x \cdot Fx)$' expresses that there is one and only one entity in F. (Similarly '$E!(\varepsilon x \cdot Fx)$' expresses that there is at least one selected entity having F, and this of course is logically equivalent to '$(Ex)Fx$' itself.) Virtual-class and -relation existence are something else again. Let '$\exists_{VC}!F$' express that the virtual class F is not null or empty, and '$\exists_{VR}!R$' similarly for the virtual (dyadic) relation R.

Should '$E!$', '$\exists_{VC}!$' and $\exists_{VR}!$' here be regarded as *predicates*? Well, not strictly, for they are defined only contextually in special ways. However, it is a trivial matter to transform them into existence-predicates as follows. Let $\{x \ni —x—\}$ be the virtual class of all entities x such that $—x—$, where '$—x—$' is a sentential form containing 'x' as its only free variable. Then, similarly, let $\{F \ni —F—\}$ be the virtual class of virtual classes satisfying the given condition. ('F' is of course a virtual-class constant, but it may be employed here as a kind of variable *manqué*, with no quantifiers upon it.) Then '$\{F \ni —F—\}G$' expresses that G is a member of the given virtual class of virtual classes, and this, by a principle of abstraction, is logically equivalent to '$—G—$', '$—F—$' and '$—G—$' differing appropriately. We may then define

$$\text{'}\exists_{VC}! \text{'} \quad \text{as} \quad \text{'}\{F \ni (Ex)Fx\}\text{'},$$

gaining a (second-order) predicate for virtual-class existence. And similarly for the relational

$$\text{'}\exists_{VR}!\text{'} \quad \text{defined as} \quad \text{'}\{R \ni (Ex)(Ey)Rxy\}\text{'},$$

where 'R' is a relational constant picked out in advance with the abstract containing it suitably defined. To say then that a virtual

---

[5] On virtual classes and relations, see especially the author's *Belief, Existence, and Meaning* (New York University Press, New York: 1969), Chapter VI.

class G exists is to say that it is a member of the class of classes $\exists_{VC}!$. And similarly for relations.

Finally the descriptional '$E!$' may even be regarded as a second-order predicate as applied to virtual classes. Thus

$$\text{'}E_\iota!\text{'}\quad\text{may be taken as short for}$$

$$\text{'}\{G \ni (Ex)(Gx \cdot (\forall y)(Gy \supset y = x))\}\text{'}.$$

And similarly

$$\text{'}E_\varepsilon!\text{'}\quad\text{for}\quad\text{'}\{G \ni (Ex)Gx\}\text{'}.$$

Then '$E_\iota!F$' expresses that there is one and only one member of F, the '$E_\iota!$' being a special existence predicate applicable to virtual classes and expressing "has one and only one member." Note that the predicate here incorporates 'ι' as a subscript, and is not a predicate significant with '$(\iota x \cdot Fx)$' as argument. The latter expression is not strictly a term anyhow but is merely defined contextually. And we could now define

$$\text{'}E!(\iota x \cdot Fx)\text{'}\quad\text{as}\quad\text{'}E_\iota!F\text{'},$$

if such a notation is desired.

Note that all the existence predicates introduced thus far are second-order predicates[6] and that no existence predicate for individuals has been introduced. One convenient way of gaining this latter is by introducing the null individual N as that entity that is a part of all entities, where "part of" is construed in the sense of the calculus of individuals.[7] ('xPy' expresses that x is a part of y.) To say that an entity is not identical with N is then to say of course that it exists. Thus we may let

$$\text{'}\exists_I\text{'}\quad\text{abbreviate}\quad\text{'}\{y \ni \sim y = N\}\text{'},$$

gaining in the definiendum a first-order predicate for the existence of individuals. To say then that $\exists_I!x$ is, to say that x is a member of the class $\exists_I!$, the class of individuals not identical with N, or, by abstraction, that x is not N.

Note that '$\exists_I!(\iota x \cdot Fx)$' is now defined, where in general '$G(\iota x \cdot Fx)$' is. We have been presupposing all along, of course, that

---

[6] The talk of existence as a second-order virtual class of virtual classes or virtual relation between virtual relations, is of course reminiscent of Frege and Russell. The reflections here are thought to exonerate fully the view that existence may be adequately handled as a predicate.

[7] Cf. the author's "Of Time and the Null Individual," *The Journal of Philosophy*, vol. 62 (1965), pp. 42–51.

this latter is short for '$(Ex)(Fx \cdot Gx \cdot (\forall y)(Fy \supset y = x))$'. It might obtain that $E_\iota!F$ but that $\sim\exists_I!(\iota x \cdot Fx)$, the one member of F being the null individual. To assure that the one individual in F is not the null individual we should write '$(E_\iota!F \cdot \exists_I! (\iota x \cdot Fx))$' or else $(E_\iota!\{x \ni (Fx \cdot \sim x = N)\})$'. The advantage of the notation '$\exists_I!(\iota x \cdot Fx)$' is that it allows the first-order predicate of existence for individuals to apply to described entities, just as '$G(\iota x \cdot Fx)$' allows first-order predicates to apply to such.

All of the existence predicates introduced thus far are in the logical tense of timelessness, so to speak. But "exists" as a word of natural language in many of its uses occurs only as tensed. How now can we extend our system so as to be able to handle tensed predicates of existence?

Let us turn to event logic and make use of *gerundive* or *event-descriptive* predicates. Let 'e', 'e_1', 'e''', and so on, be the event variables. Where 'Q' is a primitive one-place predicate applicable to individuals, we now let '$\langle Q \rangle$' be a one-place gerundive predicate applicable to events. Thus where 'Qx' expresses that x is a member of Q, '$\langle Q \rangle e$' expresses that e is a Q-ing, a process or event or state or whatever. Also let 'e By$_{\text{Agent}} x$' express that e has x as agent, or takes place with x as agent. To say that Qx is then to say that $(Ee)(\langle Q \rangle e. \ e \ \text{By}_{\text{Agent}} x).$[8] Thus to say, tenselessly, that Theaetetus walks is to say that there is a walking by or on the part of Theaetetus as agent. The prepositional relation required here will depend upon the gerundive predicate. To say that Theaetetus is happy is to say that there is a happy or happiness-state belonging to or possessed by Theaetetus. Here the Of-relation of possession is the relevant one. And so on.

Along with the gerundive predicates a temporal *before-than* relation B may be introduced. Then '$e_1 B e_2$' is to express that e_1 takes place or occurs wholly before e_2 does. For the theory of tense some locution for the deictic "now" is needed. Let 'sp Now e' express that the speaker takes e to occur during whatever time-span his relevant use of "now" covers, a split second, a moment, an hour, a day, and so on. The full theory of "now" is complicated and requires a very considerable discussion, but the simple locution 'sp Now e' must suffice for present purposes.[9] It is clear that with 'B' and 'Now' available, the means are at hand for expressing tense.

---

[8] Cf. Hans Reichenbach, *Elements of Symbolic Logic* (The Macmillan Co., New York: 1947), p. 271.

[9] For deeper discussion, see the author's "On the Logic of 'Now'," to appear.

And concerning both of these, of course, suitable meaning postulates must be given.

Nothing has been said in the foregoing as to how the identity of individuals is handled. Let us suppose it to have been taken as a primitive. A weak kind of identity may be defined as mutual part-to-whole, which we may aptly call *mereological* identity. If two individuals are identical, they are then mereologically identical, but not necessarily conversely, as we shall see in a moment.

Among the prepositional relations two are of especial interest, *From* and *To*. The most important aspect of a dyadic relation is its *sense* or direction. The relation goes *from* an object *to* an object. To say that John salutes Mary is to say that a saluting takes place from John to Mary. Equivalently we can say here that John is the *agent* of the saluting and Mary the *patient*. Let '*e* From *x*' and '*e* To *y*' express in very general terms what is desired here.[10] Given a dyadic relation we have then in general that

$$(\forall x)(\forall y)(xRy \equiv (Ee)(\langle R \rangle e \cdot e \text{ From } x \cdot e \text{ To } y)).$$

Even the mereological identity relation may be subjected to this kind of an analysis. To say that $x = y$ is to say that there is an identity-state going *from x to y*. Because of the symmetry of identity, the 'from' and 'to' here may of course be interchanged.

Let

      '*e* Before now'   abbreviate   '$(Ee')(sp \text{ Now } e' \cdot eBe')$'

and

      '*e* After now'   abbreviate   '$(Ee')(sp \text{ Now } e' \cdot e'Be)$'.

To say that *e* Before now is to say that *e* takes place wholly before some event the speaker takes as occurring now. And similarly for "After."

We are now in a position to provide tensed predicates for the various kinds of existence introduced above. Let us consider first existence for individuals. For this a few preliminary notions are needed. In addition to the mereology for individuals, a mereology for events must be provided. Thus we allow a null event, sums of events, and so on. Also let '$\langle x \rangle e$' express that *e* is a state of or an event happening to the individual *x*. Also we may define

'e TP e''' as '$((Ee'')(Ee''')(eBe'' \cdot e' = (e \cup e'')) \vee (e''Be \cdot eBe''' \cdot e'$

     $= (e'' \cup e \cup e''')) \vee (e''Be \cdot e' = (e'' \cup e)) \vee e = e')$',

[10] See the author's "On Some Prepositional Relations," in *The Logical Enterprise*, the Fitch *Festschrift* (Yale University Press, New Haven: 1975), pp. 51–59.

expressing that e is a *temporal part* of e', that is, that the time of e (so to speak) is a part of the time of e''. (The '$\cup$' here is the sign for the summation of events.) An e is then said to be *momentary* provided it is non-null and is a temporal part of all its non-null parts. Let NE be the null event. Then clearly

'Mom e' may abbreviate '$(\sim e = \text{NE} \cdot (\forall e')((e' \text{ TP } e \cdot \sim e' =$

NE$) \supset e$ TP $e'))$'.

Then individuals x and y may be said to be *cotemporal* as follows.

'x CoTemp y' abbreviates '$((\forall e)((\text{Mom } e \cdot \langle x \rangle e) \supset (Ee')$

$(\text{Mom } e' \cdot \langle y \rangle e' \cdot \sim eBe' \cdot \sim e'Be)) \cdot (\forall e)$

$((\text{Mom } e \cdot \langle y \rangle e) \supset (Ee')(\text{Mom } e' \cdot \langle x \rangle e' \cdot \sim eBe' \cdot \sim$

$e'Be)))$'.

Thus x and y are cotemporal provided for every momentary state or event of the one, there is a corresponding simultaneous momentary state or event of the other. Also we need notion of a *temporal slice* or total cross-section of an individual. We let

'x TS1 y'   abbreviate   '$(xPy \cdot (\forall z)((z \text{ CoTemp } x \cdot zPy) \supset zPx))$'.

Thus x is a temporal slice of y if it is a part of y and such that all parts of y cotemporal with it are parts of it.

Clearly we may now let

'$\exists_\text{I}^{now}!$' be short for '$\{x \ni (Ey)(y \text{ TS1 } x \cdot \sim yPN \cdot$

$\sim(Ee)(\langle = \rangle e' \cdot e \text{ From } y \cdot e \text{ To } N \cdot sp \text{ Now } e))\}$'.

Thus to say that x *now exists*, or $\exists_\text{I}^{now}!x$, roughly, is to say that there is no identity state from some non-null temporal slice of x to N during what the speaker takes as now, in other words, roughly, that some non-null temporal slice of x is not now identical with N. And similarly for the past and future. Let

'$\exists_\text{I}^{past}!$'   abbreviate   '$\{x \ni (Ey)(y \text{ TS1 } x \cdot \sim yPN \cdot \sim(Ee)$

$(\langle = \rangle e \cdot e \text{ From } y \cdot e \text{ To } N \cdot e \text{ Before now})\}$'

and

'$\exists_\text{I}^{future}!$'   abbreviate   '$\{x \ni (Ey)(y \text{ TS1 } x \cdot \sim yPN \cdot \sim(Ee)$

$(\langle = \rangle e \cdot e \text{ From } y \cdot e \text{ To } N \cdot e \text{ After now})\}$'.

Note that these definitions allow us consistently to ascribe existence in the past to an object, but to deny present and future existence, to deny past existence, but to ascribe present and future existence, and so on. Any theory of tense for existence predicates must, it would seem, be such as to allow this. Thus "St. Paul's Cathedral existed [or was in existence] yesterday" is compatible "St. Paul's exists today." To say the former is to say that at least one non-null temporal slice of it existed yesterday, and to say the latter is to say that some non-null temporal slice of it exists today, these slices, it so happens, not being the same.

For tensed descriptional existence we may let

'E_ι^{now}!'   abbreviate   '$\{G \ni (Ex)(Gx \cdot \exists_I^{\text{now}}!x \cdot (\forall y)(Gy \supset y = x))\}$',

and similarly

'E_ι^{past}!'   abbreviate   '$\{G \ni (Ex)(Gx \cdot \exists_I^{\text{past}}!x \cdot (\forall y)(Gy \supset y = x))\}$',

and

'E_ι^{future}!'   abbreviate   '$\{G \ni (Ex)$

$$\cdot (Gx \cdot \exists_I^{\text{future}}!x \cdot (\forall y)(Gy \supset y = x))\}'.$$

Thus, to say that the author of such and such a book exists now, is to ascribe the second-order predicate 'E_ι^{now}!' to the class of authors of that book. And similarly for 'E_ι^{past}!' and 'E_ι^{future}'.

Just as statements of the existence of individuals are tensed, so in ordinary language are statements of the existence of virtual classes and relations. However a thesis of reducibility here seems to obtain. It is very likely that the tensing of such statements can always be achieved by tensing, so to speak, the individuals in the classes said to exist, or which are the relata of the relations said to exist. Thus to say that there were Emperors of Rome, or that the class of Roman Emperors existed, is to say that at least some of its members were in the past, perhaps even all of them. Thus we may let

'$\exists_{\text{VC}}^{\text{past}}$!'   be short for   '$\{G \ni (Ex)(\exists_I^{\text{past}}!x \cdot Gx)\}$'.

Similarly

'$\exists_{\text{VC}}^{\text{now}}$!'   is short for   '$\{G \ni (Ex)(\exists_I^{\text{now}}!x \cdot Gx)\}$'

and

'$\exists_{\text{VC}}^{\text{future}}$!'   is short for   '$\{G \ni (Ex)(\exists_I^{\text{Future}}!x \cdot Gx)\}$'.

And likewise for virtual relations, so that

'$\exists_{VR}^{past}!$' abbreviates '$\{R \ni (Ex)(Ey)((\exists_I^{past}!x \lor \exists_I^{past}!y) \cdot xRy)\}$'.

It seems sufficient to have at least one of x and y exist in the past here, perhaps both. The relation of being *father of* existed at such and such a past time even if some offspring are still alive. On the other hand, it seems best to let

'$\exists_{VR}^{now}!$' abbreviate '$\{R \ni (Ex)(Ey)(\exists_I^{now}!x \cdot \exists_I^{now}!y \cdot xRy)\}$'

Here both x and y are required to exist now. The relation of being *president of* exists now only if there is both something present to be a president of and a present president of it. But '$\exists_{VR}^{future}!$' would seem to require the weaker requirement of having at least one of the relata exist, so that

'$\exists_{VR}^{future}!$' may abbreviate '$\{R \ni (Ex)(Ey)((\exists_I^{future}!x \lor \exists_I^{future}!y)$

$\cdot xRy)\}$'.

These three predicates, it would seem, are not particularly useful, because we rarely ascribe existence to relations in ordinary language. In any case, it is not easy to give "natural" examples of the various existence predicates introduced without bringing in a great deal more. The reason is that these notions occur in ordinary language primarily in sentential contexts containing additional phrases, and these sentences in turn are embedded in wider contexts of use, in conversations, in whole paragraphs, and so on. One cannot ordinarily give a logical form to an English sentence such as "John exists" or "John is" *simpliciter*, without taking account also of the context in which it occurs. These contexts usually contain at least an adverbial specifying the time, as already suggested.

Incidentally, throughout we have been speaking of dyadic relations only. Existence predicates for relations of higher degree may also be introduced, and might well turn out to have some interesting properties if looked at *from close to*.

Thus far attention has been confined exclusively to the existence of individuals, of virtual classes of them, and of dyadic relations between them. The individuals have been assumed to be entities to which the calculus of individuals is applicable, with its part-whole relation. No matter how catholic one's list of individuals may be, the "abstract" objects of mathematics and of theoretical physics are not to be found among them. The language of theoretical science is thus in effect excluded from the foregoing considerations. This is of course a most grave and grievous exclusion, and must be remedied post haste.

In a forthcoming paper a method of formulating what is essentially the Zermelo–Skolem–Fraenkel set theory upon a foundation in the calculus of individuals has been outlined.[11] The method seems to have some kinship with the Scotistic theory of universals. The theory developed is a kind of *moderate* realism. There are no variables but the ones for individuals and no new entities such as sets, or anything of the kind, are admitted. But the effect of having them is achieved by using suitable *sums* of individuals instead, precisely the sums of the calculus of individuals. A suitable sum is both an *unum in multis*, being a compound individual, and also an *unum de multis* in consisting of just certain individuals that are parts of it *in certain ways*. A new relational primitive is needed, very much like the 'ε' of membership of set theory, to enable us to handle the *unum de multis* suitably.

Let 'x Haec y' express that x is an *haecceity* of y, that is, one of the individuals of which y is a sum. Of course y may be a sum of individuals in various ways, and in any specific instance we must write out an expression for y. Within set theory we write out an expression for a set in terms of abstraction, say '$\hat{x}$—x—', in order to be able to determine its membership, namely, just the entities x such that —x—, where '—x—' is a sentential form containing free occurrences of the one variable 'x' built up from atomic ε-formulae in the usual way by means of negation, disjunction, and quantification. Whether '$\hat{x}$—x—' really designates a set or not will depend of course upon how it is built up. So here, a suitable way of expressing abstraction must be found—*quasi-abstraction*, let us call it—within the notation of the calculus of individuals, so that it can be determined whether x Haec y or not, where in place of 'y' we insert a quasi-abstract.

Let '$(x1$—x—$)$' stand for the sum of all atomic elements such that —x—, '—x—' being a suitable sentential form. An atomic element, recall, is a non-null entity that is a part of all its non-null parts.[12] Consider now the sum $(x1(Ey)(xPy \cdot$ —y—$))$, of all atoms that are parts of some y such that —y—. The '—y—' here is a sentential form built up from atomic formulae of the form 'x Haec z' in the

---

[11] "On Common Names and Mathematical Scotism," *Ratio*, to appear.

[12] Cf. Alfred Tarski, "On the Foundations of Boolean Algebra," in his *Logic, Semantics, Metamathematics* (Clarendon Press, Oxford: 1956), p. 334. Cf. also C. S. Peirce, *Collected Papers* (Harvard University Press, Cambridge: 1931–1958), Vol. 3, §216.

usual way. Suitable laws of abstraction, rather restricted ones actually, are postulated concerning these sums.

It is also useful to observe that one and the same expression may be regarded as *designating* a given sum as an *unum in multis*, but as *denoting* just the individuals which are the haecceities of that sum taken as an *unum de multis* and as stipulated by that expression. This, in a nutshell, is the rendering here of the famous "formal distinction" of Duns Scotus. The word "man" designates the mereological sum of all men, this sum being an *unum in multis*, but denotes each and every individual man, the sum then being the *unum de multis* stipulated by "man."

To illustrate the method, let us glance at one of the axioms of the Zermelo-Skolem-Frankel system, to see what it looks like in the present version. Let us consider, say, the Power Axiom, that given any set, there is a set whose members are just its subsets. This becomes here the principle that

$$(\forall x)(\forall y)(y \text{ Haec } (z\,1(Ew)(zPw \cdot (\forall u)(u \text{ Haec } w \supset u \text{ Haec } x))) \equiv$$

$$(\forall u)(u \text{ Haec } y \supset u \text{ Haec } x)).$$

Note that this principle is actually only a restricted abstraction principle, the quasi-abstract '$(z\,1(Ew\text{———})$' being available primitively as a term. In a similar way the other axioms may be formulated, some of them, such as the *Aussonderungsaxiom*, the *Ersetzungsaxiom*, and the *Fundierungsaxiom*, only as schemata.

We could now add all of the axioms of the Z-S-F system to the axioms and meaning postulates of the foregoing. It seems preferable, however, in accord with *moderate* realism, to take these axioms rather as hypotheses where needed. Russell, it will be recalled, used such a device in *Principia Mathematica* with regard to the Axiom of Infinity and the Multiplicative Axiom. Unable to decide whether they are true or not—and anyhow they are not principles of logic, he thought—he took them as antecedents to conditionals, the consequents of which are provable only if they are assumed. Let us perform a similar trick here. Let '$ZSF1$', '$ZSF2$', . . . , '$ZSF14$' abbreviate the fourteen axioms needed. Suppose $ZSF12$, $ZSF13$, and $ZSF14$ are respectively the *Aussonderungsaxiom*, the *Ersetzungsaxiom*, and the *Fundierungsaxiom*. Each of these schemata provides an infinity of axioms. For example, the *Aussonderungsaxiom* is to the effect that

$$(\forall x)(\forall y)(y \text{ Haec } (z\,1(Ew(zPw \cdot Fw \cdot w \text{ Haec } x))$$

$$\equiv (Fy \cdot y \text{ Haec } x)),$$

for every virtual-class expression 'F' built up in a proper way in terms of 'Haec'. We may thus let '$ZSF12_F$' be the name of the instance of $ZSF12$ for F. And similarly then we may write '$ZSF13_F$' and '$ZSF14_R$' for appropriate instances of the other schemata.

The theorems of classical mathematics, as formulated in this version of the Zermelo set theory, may now be written in the form

$$\text{'}ZSF_{F_1,...,F_n,R_1,...,R_k} \supset \underline{\hspace{2em}}\text{'}$$

where '$ZSF_{F_1,...,F_n,R_1,...,R_k}$' is short for the conjunction of any of $ZSF1$–$ZSF14$, or instances of such in the case of the schemata, that are needed for the proof of '——'. In this way we do not commit ourselves as to the truth of the hypothesis, but we do not throw classical mathematics to the winds either, as some are wont to do. Also we leave open that alternative set theories, with alternative axioms, may serve just as well. There are no sets, according to the kind of formulation here, but only individuals and sums of them. The quasi-abstracts, and the theory governing them, provide a *modus parlando*, however, tantamount to set theory itself. This *modus parlando* should not be accepted at face value, but is useful only hypothetically where needed. We therewith do not run the risk of the danger of inconsistency inherent in any strong set theory. At best a set theory is a hypothetical construction anyhow, like theoretical science generally, and the method suggested recognizes this circumstance explicitly. And in any case, set theory is not logic or deep-structure theory, and should not be treated as such, even though of course there is close kinship.[13]

In terms of 'Haec' a strong identity relation may be introduced. Let

'$x = y$'   abbreviate   '$(\forall z)(x \text{ Haec } z \supset y \text{ Haec } z)$'.

Clearly if $x = y$ then x and y are mereologically identical but not necessarily conversely. This strong identity is equivalent to that taken as a primitive above, on suitable hypotheses.

Any theoretical science may be regarded as an applied set theory, gained by adding suitable non-logical constants and axiomatizing them appropriately. So here too we may take as hypotheses whatever assumptions are needed for some theoretical principle or statement, without committing ourselves as to the truth of either.

---

[13] For a recent discussion, see George Boolos, "On Second-order Logic," *The Journal of Philosophy*, vol. 72 (1975), pp. 509–527. For a recent philosophical discussion of set theory itself, with comments by Gödel, see Hao Wang, *From Mathematics to Philosophy* (Humanities Press, New York: 1974), VI.

The various existence predicates introduced above automatically are extended now to include existence within theoretical science, and nothing can be shown to exist that could not be shown to exist on the basis of the foregoing. But all manner of additional existence predicates of a hypothetical kind are now definable. Let Hyp_i be any i hypotheses of the quasi-set-theory here or of some theoretical science, including perhaps some hypotheses interrelating the specifically theoretical material with the foregoing mereology. These hypotheses may be either axioms or theorems. Then we may let

$$\text{`Hyp}_i\text{E}_\iota\text{!'} \quad \text{may abbreviate} \quad \text{`}\{F \ni (\text{Hyps}_i \equiv \text{E}_\iota\text{!}F)\}\text{',}$$

$$\text{`Hyp}_i\exists_{\text{VC}}\text{!'} \quad \text{may abbreviate} \quad \text{`}\{F \ni (\text{Hyps}_i \equiv \exists_{\text{VC}}\text{!}F)\}\text{',}$$

and of course

$$\text{`Hyp}_i\exists_{\text{VR}}\text{!'} \quad \text{may abbreviate} \quad \text{`}\{R \ni (\text{Hyps}_i \equiv \exists_{\text{VR}}\text{!}R\}\text{'.}$$

In each case here, 'Hyp_i' must be construed narrowly so as to be equivalent to a statement of existence.

Even tensed predicates of hypothetical existence may be introduced, many theoretical sciences of course having to do with time-flow. Indeed, there seems to be no reason even why a theory of time-flow cannot be combined with set theory, the result having perhaps some kinship with intuitionism.[14] It is doubtful, however, that such a theory would ever be needed for the study of natural language, tensed existence predicates for *virtual* class and relations already being available.

Within the quasi-set-theory, specifically set-theoretical hypothetical existence would seem to consist of either having an haecceity or being the unique entity having no haecceities. This is the kind of existence appropriate to the individuals of that theory. Thus we may introduce the predicate of existence

'$\exists_{\text{Haec}}$!' as short for
$\text{`}\{x \ni ((Ey)y \text{ Haec } x \lor (Ez)(\sim(Ew)w \text{ Haec } z \cdot x$

$= z \cdot (\forall u)(\sim(Ew)w \text{ Haec } u \supset u = z)))\}\text{'.}$

Further types of individual existence could be introduced in special sciences, depending specifically upon the hypotheses chosen.

[14] Cf. William C. Powell, "Extending Gödel's Negative Interpretation to ZF," *The Journal of Symbolic Logic*, vol. 40 (1975), pp. 221–229.

Nothing thus far has been said concerning the existence of events. The existential quantifier over such has been used above without comment. A realm of events, including states, acts, processes, and the like, is recognized, so that the various existence predicates introduced for virtual classes and relations of individuals may be extended to apply also to virtual classes and relations of events. The calculus of individuals is of course extended to events and then null event recognized. An existence predicate for events may then be introduced essentially as above for individuals. And similarly for descriptional existence. And similarly for the various tensed existence predicates.

It is interesting to note that under the primary entry for "exist" in the *O.E.D.* one reads "to have place in the domain of reality, have objective being," and under the primary entry for "be" one finds "to exist, occur, happen." The word "exist" has been construed in just this sense above, it will be recalled, for the secondary objects of the cosmos which "have place" in the domain of whatever is taken to be the really real. And note the presence of "occur" and "happen" along with "to exist" in the entry for "be." The former two words are useful in speaking of events. We tend to say that an event occurs or happens rather than that it exists. We say that World War II occurred or took place, but it would be a little odd to say that it existed.

A word or two are in order concerning intentional existence, about which nothing has been said above. Intentions may be handled here in the most concrete way by means of the Fregean *Art des Gegebenseins*.[15] The bearer of intentionality is an individual, event, virtual class, or relation taken under a given linguistic description. To accommodate such entities we move into the metalanguage and form suitable ordered couples. Consider a couple $\langle x, a \rangle$ where x is denoted by the predicate a.[16] Such a couple we might think of as a *concept*, the realm of concepts being determined by the expressive powers of the language at hand. Existential quantification over concepts may be obtained then by expressions of the form

$$'(Ex)(Ea)(\text{PredConOne } a \cdot a \text{ Den } x \cdot \text{—}\langle x, a \rangle \text{—})',$$

where '—$\langle x, a \rangle$—' is a suitable context concerning the concept $\langle x, a \rangle$, and 'PredConOne a' expresses that the a is a one-place

---

[15] See especially "Über Sinn und Bedeutung," second paragraph, and *Begsiffs-schrift*, §8.

[16] See "Events" in *Events, Reference, and Logical Form*.

predicate constant of the language, either primitive or definable. Various kinds of conceptual existence-predicates may then be defined as above, including tensed ones. Various kinds of synonymy relations may be introduced, of strength ranging from logical equivalence to willingness to paraphrase by all speakers in all contexts of use. Logical equivalence is a very weak kind of synonymy. But if all members of the speaking community are willing to paraphrase a predicate *a* as the predicate *b* in all possible contexts of use of each, we have a very strong kind of synonymy indeed between *a* and *b*. It is not clear that there are synonyms in this strong sense. The most useful kinds of synonymy are presumably to be found somewhere between these extremes. In a similar way virtual-class and virtual-relation concepts may be introduced.

Closely related with the study of tense in an ordinary language is of course what is called "aspect," which concerns the manner in which the action or state is regarded. In English there are two kinds of aspect, the perfective and the progressive. In the foregoing aspect has been disregarded altogether. The notations above are useful therefore only for handling "exists," "existed," and "will exist," but not "has existed," "had existed," "is existing," "was existing," "has been existing," "will be existing," "will have been existing," and "will have existed," and so on. The logical theory of aspect remains yet to be developed. Curiously logicians have paid little attention to it, lacking suitable notions with which to explore it. The subject is very complex, much depending upon the context of occurrence. Further discussion of the subject of aspect must await another paper.

The serious study of logical form or linguistic structure has just begun. It is now surely clear that the riches of first-order logic as extended in various appropriate directions should not be neglected by the philosophic analyst interested in language nor by the professional linguist. Whatever its defects or shortcomings, the logical theory of existence and of tense sketched above is perhaps the simplest and most extensive that has yet been put forward. In any case, it is hoped that it will be useful as a basis for further study, extension, and improvement. Logico-linguistics is after all still a babbling babe in the arms of its two parents.

Institute of Advanced Study

Indeterminacy, Inscrutability, and Ontological Relativity

GERALD J. MASSEY

1. *The Inscrutability of Indeterminacy*

THE number of interpretations of Quine's indeterminacy of translation thesis probably exceeds the number of his commentators. (In a backhanded way, this plethora of interpretations itself lends confirmation to the thesis.) That Quine should be so variously understood or misunderstood might have been expected had Quine rested content with his first formulation of the scope for empirically unconditioned variation in conceptual schemes, the formulation couched in the jargon of intuitive semantics:

> ... two men could be just alike in all their dispositions to verbal behavior under all possible sensory stimulations, and yet the meanings or ideas expressed in their identically triggered and identically sounded utterances could diverge radically, for the two men, in a wide range of cases.[1]

For, as Quine himself acknowledged, this uncritical formulation verges on meaninglessness. But Quine took pains to articulate two other formulations, to wit:

> ... the infinite totality of sentences of any given speaker's language can be so permuted, or mapped onto itself, that (*a*) the totality of the speaker's dispositions to verbal behavior remains invariant, and yet (*b*) the mapping is no mere correlation of sentences with *equivalent* sentences, in any plausible sense of equivalence however loose.[2]

and the translation formulation:

> ... manuals for translating one language into another can be set up in divergent ways, all compatible with one another. In countless places they will diverge in giving, as their respective translations of a sentence of the one language, sentences of the other language which stand to each other in no plausible sort of equivalence however loose.[3]

---

[1] W. V. Quine, *Word and Object.* (Boston: The Technology Press of M.I.T., 1960), p. 26.

[2] *Ibid.*, p. 27.

[3] *Ibid.*, p. 27.

The third formulation, the indeterminacy of translation thesis, was meant by its *realism* to give readers a sure grip on the matter, yet it has obviously failed to do so. Why?

One reason surely is the unavailability of full-blown rival translation manuals. The thesis alleges the existence, for an arbitrary language *L*, of divers manuals whose translations of *L*-sentences significantly diverge countless times and yet do equal justice to all speech dispositions. The provision of such manuals would without question promote understanding of the thesis. Yet Quine has himself despaired of exhibiting a full-blown rival to some standard manual.[4] Contemplation of the intricate network of compensatory adjustments called for by departures from a standard manual *seems* to justify his despair. In lieu of providing full-blown rival manuals Quine has done the next best thing, to sketch what such manuals might look like. But because a sketch falls short of being a blueprint, Quine's case for translational indeterminacy is not anchored in the bedrock of exhibited rival manuals. It floats rather on the epistemic swampland of contemplation of methodology. As Quine puts it, "one has only to reflect on the nature of possible data and methods to appreciate the indeterminacy."[5]

By way of sketching rival manuals for a jungle language, Quine suggests plausibly that divers manuals might translate the unsullied native's "gavagai" variously as "rabbit," "undetached rabbit part," "rabbit state," "rabbit fusion" or "rabbithood," i.e., by general terms true of different things.[6] To illustrate how ensuing compensatory adjustments might be managed, Quine invokes Japanese classifiers and the French expression *"ne ... rien."*[7] But these examples, as well as the others he gives, are unilluminating precisely where matters are obscure. They illustrate only *local* compensatory adjustments, long familiar to students of language. What needs showing is how to effect compensatory adjustments on a *global* scale, something Quine's examples fail to do. As evidence of translational indeterminacy they fare no better—they simply beg the question.

In the sequel we will vindicate Quine on the indeterminacy of translation by exhibiting a full-blown rival to the homophonic manual for a rather rich language, what Church calls an *applied*

---

[4] *Ibid.*, p. 72.
[5] *Ibid.*, p. 72.
[6] *Ibid.*, pp. 51ff.
[7] W. V. Quine. "Ontological Relativity," *The Journal of Philosophy*, vol. 65 (1968), pp. 185–212. See pp. 191ff.

first-order functional calculus with identity and modality.[8] These manuals will show how misguided are the efforts of those who hope to render translation determinate by appeal to neuro-physiological correlates of linguistic activity, as Quine opined from the outset.[9] In one possible respect only do they fail to bear out Quine's speculations. In his much-discussed paper "On the Reasons for Indeterminacy of Translation," Quine argues that translational indeterminacy is a matter of second intension.[10] Because physical theories are underdetermined even by all possible observations, we are free to translate a foreign scientist so as to make him embrace any of the incompatible physical theories supported by the observations, whichever one we may ourselves espouse. This argument "is meant to persuade anyone to recognize the indeterminacy of translation of such portions of natural science as he is willing to regard as underdetermined by all possible observations."[11] Though Quine also speaks briefly of arguments for indeterminacy based on the inscrutability of terms,[12] one is left with the impression that at its roots all interesting indeterminacy of sentence translation is a matter of second intension, as just described. But this is wrong. The indeterminacy shown by our manuals is wholly a matter of referential inscrutability.

2. *Putnam's Manuals*

Heretofore only Putnam has claimed to exhibit full-blown rival manuals of translation. He claims even more, namely to have an algorithm for generating rival manuals for an arbitrary language.[13] The truth lies somewhere between Putnam's optimism and Quine's pessimism. Rival manuals do not come as cheap as Putnam thinks, nor as dear as Quine believes.

Recall Quine's summary of the empirical constraints on translation manuals: (1) occasion sentences are translatable; (2) truth functions can be translated; and (3) stimulus analyticity and

---

[8] Alonzo Church, *Introduction to Mathematical Logic*, Vol. I. (Princeton:Princeton University Press, 1956), p. 168.

[9] *Word and Object*, p. 74.

[10] W. V. Quine. "On the Reasons for Indeterminacy of Translation," *The Journal of Philosophy*, vol. 67 (1970), pp. 178–183.

[11] *Ibid.*, p. 183.

[12] *Ibid.*, p. 183.

[13] Hilary Putnam, "The Refutation of Conventionalism," *Nous*, vol. 8 (1974), pp. 25–40. *See* pp. 28ff.

stimulus contradictoriness can be preserved.[14] Conditions (1)–(3) define the class of *genuine* translation hypotheses. These are low-level, garden-variety empirical hypotheses subject to observational confirmation and disconfirmation within normal inductive uncertainty. Translation hypotheses that go beyond (1)–(3) are said to be *hypotheses* only in an *incomplete* sense.[15] Quine calls these incomplete hypotheses *analytical hypotheses*. A typical analytical hypothesis might equate a word or other short expression of L with a word or short expression of the linguist's home language, for example "gavagai" with the term "rabbit." Beyond conformity to (1)–(3) there are no empirical constraints on the system of hypotheses, analytical as well as genuine, that make up a translational manual. Beyond conformity to (1)–(3) there is nothing empirical for these hypotheses to conform to, nothing for them to be right or wrong about. In a clear sense analytical hypotheses are counterfeit; they give only the appearance of being genuine, of conforming to something in the empty region beyond (1)–(3).

Putnam deploys conditions (1)–(3) to generate translation manuals wholesale. (Oddly, Putnam uses the term "analytical hypothesis" for the system of hypotheses, both genuine and analytical, that Quine calls a *translation manual*.[16] We defer to Quine's usage in our critique of Putnam.) For Putnam a translation manual from L to L' is a general recursive function f from L-sentences to L'-sentences such that, for any sentences S, S_1, and S_2 of L:

(1) If S is an occasion sentence, $f(S)$ is an occasion sentence that is stimulus synonymous with S;

(2) f commutes with truth functions; [for example, $f(\ulcorner S_1$ and $S_2 \urcorner) = \ulcorner f(S_1)$ and $f(S_2) \urcorner$].

(3) If S is stimulus analytic (stimulus contradictory), so is $f(S)$.[17]

For the sake of concreteness we illustrate Putnam's algorithm for English–English manuals. Let h be the homophonic manual, i.e., h is the identity function. Pick any two truth-functionally atomic standing sentences, S_1 and S_2, that are neither stimulus analytic nor

---

[14] *Word and Object*, pp. 68ff. Quine has subsequently modified his claim that truth functions are translatable. See, for example, W. V. Quine, *The Roots of Reference*, (LaSalle: Open Court Publishing Co., 1974), pp. 75ff.

[15] *Ibid.*, p. 73.

[16] "The Refutation of Conventionalism," p. 29.

[17] *Ibid.*, p. 29.

stimulus contradictory. A manual r, rival to h, may be defined thus:

(a) $r(S_1) = S_2$ and $r(S_2) = S_1$;
(b) For any truth-functionally atomic sentence S other than S_1 or S_2, $r(S) = S$;
(c) r carries truth functions into themselves. [For example, if $\phi(S_1 \ldots, S_n)$ is a truth-functional compound of $S_1, \ldots, S_n$, then $r(\phi(S_1, \ldots, S_n)) = \phi(r(S_1), \ldots, r(S_n))$.]

Putnam claims that r satisfies Quine's conditions (1)–(3) and so qualifies as a full-blown manual rival to the homophonic manual h.[18] *Pace* Putnam, we will show that r violates condition (3). To see this, consider Putnam's own choice of standing sentences S_1 and S_2.

(S_1) The distance from the earth to the sun is about 93 million miles.
(S_2) There are no rivers on Mars.

Now notice that sentence (A) is stimulus analytic,

(A) If there are no rivers on Mars, then on Mars there are no rivers.

whereas its r-translation (B) is *not* stimulus analytic.

(B) If the distance from the earth to the sun is about 93 million miles, then on Mars there are no rivers.

To appreciate that (B) is not stimulus analytic, imagine the *New York Times* to carry a front page story, with photographs, chronicling a space-probe discovery of rivers on Mars. *Times* readers versed in astronomy would then dissent from (B), where (A) would remain stimulus analytic. The point is that standing sentences that are neither stimulus analytic nor stimulus contradictory have stimulus meanings, however sparse. Hence, so long as S_1 and S_2 are not stimulus synonymous, pairs of sentences like (A) and (B) that violate condition (3) can be constructed. Nor can one sidestep this difficulty by stipulating that S_1 and S_2 be stimulus synonymous. For the resulting manuals would no longer diverge so as to qualify as rivals, because an equivalence relation (stimulus equivalence) would obtain among the translations of any given sentence.

Did we perhaps employ a double standard when we condemned Putnam's manual r for violating condition (3), i.e., for failing to preserve stimulus analyticity? Even Quine does not insist on strict

[18] *Ibid.*, p. 35.

satisfaction of (1)–(3). On the contrary, in the interest of the overall simplicity of his manual, Quine's field linguist boldly translates a stimulus analytic native sentence as "Rabbits are men reincarnate," thereby transgressing (3).[19] By contrast, Putnam's violation of (3) detracts from the simplicity of his manual r. On every relevant methodological index the homophonic manual h ties or outscores r. But to be *rivals* two manuals must not only diverge countless times; they must in addition have equally good methodological credentials (simplicity, etc.). So r fails again to be a rival to h, this time for reasons of scientific method.

Suppose contrary to fact that Putnam's manual r had qualified as a rival to h. Would r underwrite the inscrutability of reference? All the manuals sketched by Quine are word-word manuals (more accurately, short expression-short expression manuals), and for good reason. Quine wants to establish the manual relativity, hence inscrutability, of reference (or, as he sometimes calls it, the *inscrutability of terms*). He wants to show that equally good manuals may assign significantly different referents to terms, whether singular or general. Such relativity of reference cannot be exhibited by manuals that agree on those occasions, if any, when they dip beneath sentence level. Manual r never dips below sentence level, so it would appear to be of no avail in showing that reference is relative to manuals. The appearance is deceptive, however. As we will show, r induces a word-word manual r^* that diverges referentially from h.

Quine allows that a manual may translate an expression one way in one context, another way in another.[20] We capitalize upon this latitude to get r^*. Let r^* translate words homophonically unless they occur in sentences S_1 or S_2; in the latter case, the singular term "Mars" is translated as "the earth" and conversely; similarly, the general term "there are no rivers on ..." is translated as "the distance from ... to the sun is about 93 million miles" and conversely. Then an r^*-theory of reference assigns the earth as the referent of "Mars" and Mars as the referent of "the earth" *in the aforementioned contexts*, whereas our familiar h-theory of reference makes Mars and the earth the respective referents of "Mars" and "the earth" in the same contexts. Clearly, what we have just done with r could be done with any manual that diverges from h in finitely many sentential contexts. That is, we can use such a manual to induce a word-word manual that diverges referentially from h.

---

[19] *Word and Object*, p. 69.
[20] *Ibid.*, p. 69.

But is the induced manual r^* a *rival to h* (under our counterfactual assumption that r is a rival to h)? Apparently not, because r^* harbors an unredeemed complexity absent from h. Remember: only manuals that tie for methodological first place qualify as *rivals* in Quine's sense. Still, the added complexity is so miniscule relative to the manuals as wholes that one might nonetheless want to count r^* as tied with h, given that r and h are tied. Grant, then, that r^* is a rival to h. Do r^* and h together establish the inscrutability of reference? To be interesting, the thesis of the inscrutability of reference must demand much more than occasional or isolated divergence of reference; it must require *thoroughgoing referential divergence*, divergence that cannot be waved off as a mere quirk of translation. The dualistic manual d, to be presented shortly, is a word-word manual that diverges referentially *everywhere* from h. So, unlike r^*, d supports not only the indeterminacy of translation, but the added weight of the inscrutability of reference as well.

Although wrong in his claim that r is a translation manual rival to h, Putnam is right in a more important matter, namely in his charge that Quine treats conditions (1)–(3) as meaning postulates governing "translation."[21] For Quine, (1)–(3) encapsulate all the empirical constraints on translation, thereby demarcating genuine translation hypotheses from pseudo-empirical analytical hypotheses. But this construal of (1)–(3) depends on treating certain *analytical* hypotheses, those concerning assent and dissent, as if they were *genuine* hypotheses, as if there were something for them to be right or wrong about.

Quine himself recognizes that hypotheses about native signs of assent and dissent are analytical hypotheses. They differ from garden-variety analytical hypotheses only in this: they are among the earliest analytical hypotheses that the linguist advances in order to get the enterprise of radical translation off the ground.[22] *Now recognize hypotheses about assent and dissent as analytical and you no longer have any reason to suppose that an empirically adequate manual must conform to conditions* (1)–(3). Rather than argue for the empirical irrelevance of (1)–(3), we shall exhibit it directly by constructing an empirically adequate rival to h that violates all three conditions everywhere. Such is our manual d below.

---

[21] "The Refutation of Conventionalism," p. 38.

[22] See *Word and Object*, p. 30 f.; "Ontological Relativity," p. 189; *The Roots of Reference*, pp. 45ff.; and especially p. 312 of W. V. Quine, "To Hintikka," pp. 312–315 in *Words and Objections*, eds. D. Davidson and J. Hintikka (Dordrecht: Reidel Publishing Co., 1969).

3. *The Dualistic Manual*

Let L be a first-order language with identity and alethic modality but without singular terms. The absence of singular terms betokens no impoverishment. We can compensate *à la* Quine for their absence by introducing descriptions via individuating predicates. For example, the singular term "Socrates" gives way to the description "the one who socratizes" or "the one who is-identical-to-Socrates" via the concocted general term "socratizes" or the unanalyzed general term "is-identical-to-Socrates," predicates true of just one thing, Socrates.[23] Let d be the following (*dualistic*) L-L manual. Where φ is a general term, $d(\varphi)$ is the complement term of φ. That is, $d(\varphi)$ is true (false) of something just in case φ is false (true) of it. For example, whereas "rabbit" is true of rabbits according to the homophonic L-L manual h, "rabbit" is true of all and only non-rabbits according to the dualistic manual d. Similarly, '$\geq$' is true of an ordered pair $\langle a, b \rangle$ according to h just in case a is greater than or equal to b; according to d, '$\geq$' is true of $\langle a, b \rangle$ just in case a is not greater or equal to b. Quite in general, then, the d reference of a general term is the complement of its h reference. More referentially divergent manuals are scarcely conceivable! For the rest, d translates each connective or operator by its dual: negation by negation (since negation is self-dual), disjunction by conjunction, conjunction by disjunction, the existential (universal) quantifier by the universal (existential) quantifier, possibility by necessity, and necessity by possibility. Finally, the d-linguist posits assent (dissent) wherever the h-linguist posits dissent (assent).

Assume that the h-linguist and d-linguist query natives alike and consider how their respective manuals fare. To inquire whether all rabbits are vegetarians, the h-linguist asks '$(\forall x)(\sim Rx \vee Vx)$?' and is rewarded by the native's sign of assent "Yes." The d-linguist takes the native to have *dissented* from '$(\exists x)(\sim \bar{R}x \,\&\, \bar{V}x)$', as expected. (The horizontal bar over a predicate turns it into the complement term.) Suppose conversation moves from rabbits to natural numbers. To the h-linguist's question '$(\exists x)[Nx \,\&\, (\forall y)(\sim Ny \vee x \geq y)]$?', the native responds "No," thereby impressing the h-linguist with his mathematical sophistication. But the d-linguist is no less impressed, for he takes the native to have *assented* to '$(\forall x)[\bar{N}x \vee (\exists y)(\sim \bar{N}y \,\&\, x \overset{=}{\geq} y)]$'. Conversation now takes a philosophical turn. The h-linguist asks '$\Box(\forall x)(\sim Rx \vee Vx)$?'

---

[23] See W. V. Quine, *Methods of Logic*, revised edition (New York: Holt, Rinehart and Winston, 1959), p. 218 f.

and is pleased to get the response "No" that fits in with his own bias. Sharing that bias the d-linguist is equally gratified that, as he sees it, the native has assented to '$\Diamond(\exists x)(\sim\bar{R}x \, \& \, \bar{V}x)$'.

By now our examples have perhaps belabored the obvious, or at least what will be obvious to those conversant with duality. Whatever the linguists ask and however the natives respond, the h-linguist and d-linguist will be equally convinced, on equally good grounds, that their respective manuals correctly translate L. And yet the d-translation of an L-sentence will be true or false (at a world) just in case its h-translation is respectively false or true (at that world). Systematic interchange within the pairs truth-falsehood and assent-dissent guarantees that the d-manual will enjoy whatever success in the field that the h-manual meets with, and to exactly the same degree. And since each manual is as simple, parsimonious, etc. as the other, they qualify in every respect as *rival* manuals.

Nor does anything go awry when inference behavior is taken into account. Suppose, for example, that the h-linguist takes the native to have reasoned correctly from the joint assertion of '$(\forall x)$ $(\sim Rx \vee Vx)$' and '$(\exists x)Rx$' to the assertion of '$(\exists x)Vx$'. The d-linguist will understand the native to have moved, with equally impeccable logic, from the joint denial of '$(\exists x)(\sim\bar{R}x \, \& \, \bar{V}x)$' and '$(\forall x)\bar{R}x$' to the denial of '$(\forall x)\bar{V}x$'. For the d-linguist inverts assertion and denial just as he inverts assent and dissent.

It should be evident, too, that neuro-physiological investigations can never favor one manual over the other. Imagine whatever brain states, neural mechanisms, etc. you like—they will be absolutely neutral as between h and d. For whatever correlates of linguistic states, etc. you posit from the perspective of h-semantics, they will serve equally admirably as correlates from the perspective of d-semantics. Quine is absolutely right about this. The quest for neuro-physiological states and mechanisms that will render translation determinate is a colossal wild goose chase!

Reflection on duality suggests a less roundabout alternative to h than d. Let c be the *contradictory* L-L manual where, for any sentence S, $c\,(S) = \ulcorner \sim S \urcorner$, and where c inverts assent-dissent and assertion-denial exactly as d does.[24] The manual c will fare as well, both in the field and systemically, as the homophonic manual h and so qualifies as a rival to h. Hence the pair of manuals c and h

---

[24] When commenting upon the version of this paper delivered by the author on March 29, 1976 at the International Philosophy Conference in the Biltmore Hotel, New York City, Quine stated that he had known of the contradictory manual for some time, having used it as an example in courses and seminars.

instantiate Quine's indeterminacy of translation thesis, as do the pair d and h. But unlike the pair d and h, the pair c and h fail to establish the inscrutability of reference. Like Putnam's manual r, c is not a word-word manual. But unlike r, c cannot be used to induce a word-word manual that diverges referentially from h at the sub-sentential level. It seems that the roundaboutness of d is necessary to vindicate Quine on the inscrutability of reference, as well as to display the irrelevance of neurophysiology to the translational indeterminacy thesis.

4. *The Cretan Manual*

The d and h manuals incontestably instantiate the inscrutability of reference. But do they really establish the indeterminacy of translation? Someone might object that the d-linguist and the h-linguist both take the native to make the same *statements*, however differently they may translate his *sentences*. Quine should have couched his formulations of the scope for empirically unconditioned variation in conceptual schemes in terms of statements rather than sentences, or so the objection runs. For example, the mapping version (Quine's second formulation) might be recast thus: the statements of a language can be mapped onto themselves in a speech-dispositions-preserving manner in such a way that no plausible relation of equivalence, however loose, obtains among paired statements. Such an objection would be tendered only by philosophers who have no scruples about countenancing statements in their ontologies. While the number of such philosophers seems to have dwindled in recent years, it remains perhaps large enough to warrant a reply to the objection.

Consider a new manual e, to be called *the Cretan manual* ('e' for Epimenides). So far as translation of terms, connectives, and operators goes, e behaves exactly like d. But with respect to assent and dissent, assertion and denial, e behaves like h. Now the e-linguist is a very suspicious individual. He takes the natives to be asserting falsehoods whenever the h-linguist takes them to be asserting truths. Only on those rare occasions when the h-linguist thinks the natives are lying does the e-linguist take them to be speaking truthfully. Ordinarily, when a native asserts '$(\forall x)$ $(\sim Rx \vee Vx)$', the h-linguist will understand him to state truthfully that all rabbits are vegetarians, whereas the e-linguist will take the native to assert deceitfully that some rabbits are not vegetarians. The *statement* which the h-linguist takes the native to have made *contradicts* the *statement* which the *e*-linguist takes him to have made, and the same will hold for any sentence the native may assert or deny. So recasting Quine's formulations in terms of statements rather than sentences raises no bar to translational indeterminacy.

But doesn't *e* run afoul of the *sociological fact* that people by and large try to tell the truth? The question carries a false presupposition; there is no such fact to run afoul of. Note that the alleged fact is as much semantical as sociological. Modify the semantics, for example by employing a non-standard manual like *e*, and you *eo ipso* modify the "fact". The *e*-linguist can and will insist that for the most part the natives assert falsehoods, and with as much justification as the *h*-linguist has for his insistence that the natives usually speak the truth. All that favors the *h*-linguist's point of view is a certain conceit about human nature, a conceit born more of semantics than of sociology. But can't the dispute between the linguists be settled by an appeal to polygraphs or similar devices? By no means! The *e*-linguist will value polygraphs just as much for detecting veracity as the *h*-linguist will value them for detecting mendacity.

With a little imagination one can even motivate the *e*-linguist's prodigious suspicion. Imagine the natives to be Eskimos. Now the Eskimos have been so intensively studied by anthropologists, sociologists, and linguists that they may well have come to resent such intrusion into their lives, so much so that they resolved out of pique to speak falsehoods to one another most of the time, hoping thereby to confound the intruders.

5. *Inscrutability, Indeterminacy, and Relativity of Ontology*

Referential inscrutability, translational indeterminacy, and ontological relativity are often run together, despite Quine's protestations. Because they are distinct theses, it is important to appreciate their relations of independence as well as their interconnections. The Japanese classifiers show inscrutability of reference without bringing indeterminacy of (*sentence*) translation in their train.[25] The *gavagai* scenario is meant directly to show referential inscrutability and only indirectly to suggest translational indeterminacy; its implications for ontological relativity remain somewhat unclear.[26] Thanks to deferred ostension Quine's treatment of protosyntax is meant to establish all three theses, though the ground of

---

[25] "On the Reasons for Indeterminacy of Translation," p. 182.
[26] *Ibid.*, p. 182.

ontological relativity is expressly referential inscrutability, not translational indeterminacy.[27]

In conjunction with the h-manual, our d-manual and e-manual each demonstrates indeterminacy of sentence translation and inscrutability of reference. What bearing do these pairs of manuals have on the relativity of ontology? Let L be the home language of both the h-linguist and the d-linguist. To take the measure of the native's ontology, the h-linguist straightforwardly applies Quine's criterion, to be is to be the value of a bound variable, and concludes that the native's ontology is, say, very like his own, replete with vegetarian rabbits, an unending series of natural numbers, etc. The d-linguist reaches the same conclusion by a different route. Let P be the set of sentences which the native affirms, and N the set he denies, *from the point of view of the h-linguist*. Let Neg (Θ) be the set of negations of the members of the set Θ of sentences. Then, to arrive at the native's ontology$Y$, what the h-linguist does is to find a set Y of objects that as values of the bound variables make the members of the union $P \cup Neg(N)$ come out true. On the other hand the d-linguist arrives at the very same set Y through seeking an appropriate domain of individuals for $P' \cup Neg(N')$, where P' and N' are the sets of sentences that the native respectively affirms and denies *from the d-linguist's point of view*. Clearly a set of objects will do as the domain of $P \cup Neg(N)$ if and only if it will pass muster as the domain of $P' \cup Neg(N')$. Other choices than Y for the native's ontology were of course open to the d-linguist, but their availability depended in no way whatsoever upon the perverseness of his manual; they were equally available to the h-linguist. The point is this: even in an extreme case such as that presented by h and d wherein every general term and every sentence receives strikingly different interpretations, referential inscrutability and translational indeterminacy need not bring ontological relativity in their wake. The point is humdrum but worth emphasizing: even (global) inscrutability of reference does not entail ontological relativity.[28]

University of Pittsburgh

[27] *Ibid.*, p. 182f.
[28] See footnote 24 concerning the presentation of a version of this paper on March 29, 1976. The critique of Putnam's alleged algorithm for generating translation manuals was first presented by the author in a symposium on conventionalism at the 1974 meeting of the Western Division of the American Philosophical Association in St. Louis, Missouri, April 28, 1974.

APPENDIX

In a Polish paper whose title may be translated into English as "Why sentences aren't names," *Studia Semiotyczne,* vol. 3 (1972), Peter Geach devises an ingenious English-Unglish dictionary based on duality. Briefly put, an Unglish sentence is the dual of the corresponding English sentence. Geach's English-Unglish dictionary differs from my dualistic manual in only two respects: first, there is no explicit interchange of assertion and denial; second, his dictionary applies to even richer languages, ones boasting oblique contexts. Geach uses his dictionary to dramatize how differently names and sentences behave under duality and concludes therefrom that they belong to different syntactical categories. I am indebted to Professor Geach for calling my attention to his fascinating paper in October 1976, and for sending me an expanded English translation of it.

The Equivocality of Existence

NICHOLAS RESCHER

I. *Is Existence a Univocal or an Equivocal Conception?*

THERE is no denying that many different sorts of things exist. And there is also no denying that they exist in many different sorts of ways. But is the *existence* at issue in these different contexts always the same? Is *the same idea* operative when we say different sorts of things "exist"—do they "exist" in the same *sense* of this philosophically crucial terms?

The issue comes down to this: Can one give a strictly *uniform* account in explicating wherein the existence of different sorts of things lies? Or does the meaning-analysis of the notion of existence lead to different destinations in different settings? Is existence a univocal conception or is it equivocal, so that the different uses of "exists" are unified only by a "family resemblance"? These questions define the problem-area of the present discussion.

II. *Particulars and Universals*

In philosophical analysis it is often profitable to start with the historical lay of the land. The mainstream of logical tradition since Aristotle's day agrees on two points of ontological theory:

(1) that it is necessary to distinguish between items of substantially different sorts, and at the very least between:(i) *things* in the most basic, preeminent and primary sense of the term, viz., *particulars* or *concreta* (Aristotle's *primary* substances), and (ii) "things" in a more extended sense, namely those items which are correlative with things of the former sort, namely the properties, attributes, relations, numbers, actions, activities, dispositions, etc. of these things. All such concreta-pertaining items might be said to stand in the OF-relationship to things of the former sort, as properties, etc., *of* them. These are the *universals* or traditional *abstracta* (Aristotle's *secondary* substances), which qualify or characterize things of the former sort (particulars).

(2) that the conception of existence does not apply to particulars alone, but also to the "things" which are correlative with them. Existence is thus a *transcategorematic* feature that

57

operates not only in the category of (primary) substance, but in the other categories as well.

These considerations give special point to our initial problem. They confront us directly with the key question of whether existence is uniform as between particulars and universals. Is the existence of "things" that are not *things* (in the narrow sense of *concrete* things)—the existence of universals in short—to be understood in the same way as the existence of particulars?[1]

III. *The Construction of Existence in the Case of Concrete Individuals and that of Universals*

Let us begin with the existence of particulars. From the aspect of the "logical analysis" of the matter, this issue of particular individuals and their existence is relatively straightforward. For it is precisely these which, on the standard and customary approach, constitute the domain of our quantifiers $\forall$ and $\exists$ (general and "existential," respectively). This being so, one can proceed to achieve a logical explanation of particular-existence in quantificational terms in a relatively straightforward way:

(1) $E!x$ iff $(\exists y)(y = x)$

The validation of this formula will, of course, hinge crucially on the character of the membership-criterion for the domain of quantification.[2] But if we adopt the more or less customary stance that this pivotal criterion comes to *actual existence as a concrete particular*, then (1) is clearly, nay almost trivially, in order.[3]

---

[1] Indeed some would hold that it is senseless to speak of the existence of universals—what sense is there in claiming that the color red exists: surely a nonexistent color is a *contradictio in adjecto*. Such a view overlooks the fact that many properties are in themselves contingent, e.g., the rights, duties, and obligations of people, which endow them with properties which themselves come into being and pass away.

[2] Specifically, if "real existence" is *not* built into this formula then (1) engenders the now undesirable consequence $(\forall x)E!x$, i.e., the claim "*Everything* exists." Cf. the author's "On the Logic of Existence and Denotation," *The Philosophical Review*, vol. 68 (1959), pp. 157–180.

[3] The seemingly plausible rival formula

(1') $E!x$ iff there is some property ϕ such that ϕx

will not do. For nonexistent individuals can also have properties, although some logicians have thought otherwise, adopting the principle *nihil sunt nullae proprietatis*. However, this position involves serious problems. Cf. the author's *Essays in Philosophical Analysis* (Pittsburgh, 1969), pp. 73 ff. To meet such difficulties some logicians propose to modify (1) by adding special restrictions on the property ϕ at issue. Henry Leonard, "The Logic of Existence," *Philosophical Studies*, vol. 7 (1956), pp. 49–64, for example, insists that ϕ be a *contingent* property.

But now what of universals—say properties and relations, for example. Can we not settle the issue of uniformity in an affirmative sense by going to the following parallel existential formula:

(2) $E! \phi$ iff $(\exists \psi)(\psi = \phi)$

One certainly *can* make this move, but this time the matter cannot be permitted to rest here. For now we cannot take for granted the unproblematic givenness of a domain of quantification encompassing such *abstracta*. The membership-criterion of the domain itself becomes a far more problematic issue.

Perhaps the simplest suggestion to be made here is this: A property exists (*qua* property) if it is a characterizing feature of some extant individual:[4]

(3) $E! \phi$ if $(\exists x)\phi x$

This suggestion may be useful as a first approximation, but it is unacceptably oversimple as it stands. There can, of course, be properties, perfecly genuine and "real" properties, that are not actually exemplified in nature. The range of the properties of things is not to be determined solely by *actual encounter* but is a matter of the *theoretical systematization* and rounding off of manifest data. On a modest scale, think of Hume's famous example of the missing shade of blue. A more complex case is that of unrealized values of continuously parametrized properties (like height or weight or temperature) in a world, as we may suppose it, of finitely many objects. Or again, think of the broad feline smile of the cheshire cat. Such examples clearly show the implausibility of maintaining the nonexistence of unexemplified properties. Properties must—to exist *qua* properties—clearly *admit* of exemplification, but they need surely not be exemplified. (Many philosophical doctrines embody such a view—that of Leibniz preeminently. And compare also Santayana's important—even if controversial—conception of unenacted essences.[5])

---

[4] *Ibid.*

[5] See the articles on Santayana in *The Journal of Philosophy*, vol. 51 (1954), pp. 29–64. ("Santayana at Harvard," by C. I. Lewis, pp. 29–31; Donald C. Williams, "Of Essence and Existence and Santayana," pp. 31–42; F. A. Ollafson, "Skepticism and Animal Faith," pp. 42–46; Ernest Nagel, "Some Gleanings from The Life of Reason," pp. 46–49; J. H. Randall, Jr., "George Santayana—Naturalizing the Imagination," pp. 50–52; Justus Buchler, "One Santayana or Two?," pp. 52–57; Daniel Cory, "God or the External World," pp. 56–61; Irwin Erdman, "Philosopher as Poet," pp. 62–64.) For modern discussions of cognate views see Nicholas Rescher, "Definitions of 'Existence'," *Philosophical Studies*, vol. 8 (1957), pp. 65–80, and Jack Kaminsky, *Language and Ontology* (Carbondale and Edwardsville, 1969).

In the interests of achieving an adequate analysis of property-existence we are accordingly forced to shift our focus from actuality to possibility, from (3) to

$$(4) \qquad\qquad E!\phi \quad \text{iff} \quad \Diamond(\exists x)\phi x$$

For a property to exist, it suffices for it to be a *possible* rather than an *actual* feature of something: it need not be "enacted" or actually exemplified.[6]

Even this improved version may not be quite unproblematic—it may well yet need some further refinements of detail.[7] But it does at any rate suffice to make the point that for universals to exist *sui generis, qua* universals, they need not be instantiated; it is sufficient if they are *instantiable*. Existence in this connection—in the context of universals—has an inherently possibilistic aspect that sets it clearly apart from the emphatically actualistic mode of existence operative at the level of particulars (*concreta*). Particular-thing existence is correlative with actuality; universal–abstract existence is correlative with possibility.

These considerations clearly point towards a negative answer to our initial question of the univocality of "exists." For if one sort of explicative analysis is in order with regard to the existence of particular individuals (namely an actualistic one), and another rather different explicative analysis is in order with regard to the existence of such universals as properties (namely possibilistic ones), then it emerges that the conception of existence will have to be regarded as equivocal. Insofar as distinctly different items of conceptual machinery must be employed in giving an appropriate construction for "existence" in these two different settings, the conception is discontinuous across these areas. One is well-advised to adopt some such distinction as that espoused by Charles S. Peirce between *"existence"*-in-the-narrow-sense, namely the mode of being of individuals, and *"reality,"* the mode of being generals.[8] And the closer we consider this matter of the equivocality of existence, the more drastic it becomes.

---

[6] It becomes necessary in this context to distinguish $\Diamond(\exists x)\phi x$ from $(\exists x)\Diamond\phi x$, recognizing the clear difference between a *possibility for a real thing* on the one hand and a *real possibility for a thing* on the other. (Ruth Barcan Marcus has driven this home.) This breaks the link with particular-existence altogether. See Nicholas Rescher, *A Theory of Possibility* (Oxford, 1975).

[7] See the discussions cited in footnotes 2 and 3 above.

[8] Again, Henry Leonard (*op. cit.*) distinguishes between *singular* existence as applicable to individuals and *general* existence as applicable to universals.

IV. Higher-Order Universals; Laws and Dispositions

The dichotomy between particulars and universals needs further development. More subtle distinctions must be drawn. We can proceed to exfoliate the type-hierarchy of higher-order universals by the following recursive process:

Type-level

0 (particulars)	*p*-particulars
1 (ground-level universals)	OF-correlates (properties, relations, etc.) of *p*-particulars—i.e., all their various characteristics
i [*i* ≥ 2] (higher-level universals)	OF-correlates of type *i* − 1 (and perhaps also lower-type) items

The three corresponding cases—viz., 0, 1, and $i(\geq 2)$—call for three rather different constructions (explicative analyses) of the concept of existence:

(i) At type-level 0 the operative sense of "exists" is such that an appropriate analysis can take the form:

$$E!x \quad \text{iff} \quad (\exists y)(y = x)$$

The crucial distinction here is that between *actual* existence and merely hypothetical "existence" *sub ratione possibilitatis* (as Leibniz put it)[9]—between the "domain of discourse" and the "domain of quantification," with authentic existents alone (presumably) constituting the latter.

(ii) At type level 1 we come to the existence of the OF-correlates of ground-floor particulars. Specifically in the case of property-existence we have it that—since actual exemplification is *not* the issue—this takes an emphatically possibilistic turn:

$$E!\phi \quad \text{iff} \quad \Diamond(\exists x)\phi x \quad \text{iff} \quad (\Sigma x)\phi x.[10]$$

Strictly analogous analyses hold for relations, etc.

(iii) At the higher type levels (those ≥ 2) existence appertains to the OF-correlates of items of the lower type level(s).

[9] Note that here alone, at the level of *actualia* is there any room for *contingent* existence. At all the other levels, existence is in fact inherently possibilistic and necessitarian. The medieval principle *a posse ad esse non valet consequentia* holds in the category of *concreta* (particulars) but fails in that of *abstracta* (*universals*).

[10] Note the different (nonactualistic) mode of possible-individual quantification at issue here. This last equivalence rests on the (by no means trivial) principle that every possible feature of something is the feature of a possible something. For this principle and the assumptions on which it rests see the author's *A Theory of Possibility* (*op. cit.*).

Specifically in the case of higher-level *properties* we can capture what is at issue by means of the trans-level formula:

$E! \phi$ iff$(\exists \psi)[\phi(\psi) \& T(\psi)]$, where T represents a type-level condition upon ψ.[11]

Again, analogous analyses hold for relations, etc.[12]

We arrive at the upshot that three distinct modes of existence are at issue with respect to (i) particulars, (ii) (ground-level) universals, and (iii) higher-level universals, respectively. We must resign ourselves to recognizing existence as a distinctly pluralistic, inherently diversified conception. Emphatically different logical mechanisms are needed for the analysis at the three levels—viz.: ordinary existential quantification over individuals, existential quantification with respect to *possibilia* (or some comparable modalized device), and existential quantification with respect to *abstracta*. Thus considering that different notions calling for distinct (nonuniform) explications are at issue, it emerges different senses of existence operate at the various type-level strata. The prospect of a rigid univocality cannot be realized.

And even this account is an oversimplification. For when one regards—as one should—dispositions and laws in the light of property-analogous features (OF-correlates) of real individuals, but ones whose explication takes the possibilistic turn in the direction of *physical or natural* modalities rather than logical modalities, then one is brought to admit yet another mode of existence. The "existence" of dispositional properties and lawful relationships calls for an explication which, in involving *physical* modalities, once again differs radically in its conceptual make-up.

V. *Genus-Relative Existence*

And even this is not the end of the matter. There is yet another mode of "existence" which is quite distinct from any of the preceding.

[11] This type-level restriction can, in principle, be eliminated under suitable assumptions (such as an axiom of reducibility).

[12] One could try to maintain a distinct mode of existence for every type-level. But this seems not only uneconomical but (more seriously) unnecessary, given the fact that the same definitional pattern is uniformly operative throughout, since all of them answer to the same recursive pattern. On the other hand, it would seem implausible—given the very different explicative machinery involved—to consolidate the case of all types >0 into one single category of general existence.

Consider locutions such as:

There is a possible (i.e., *merely* possible, possible but nonexistent) individual x which meets the condition C: $C(x)$. Symbolically this could be cast in terms of a special "existential" quantifier: $(\Sigma x)C(x)$.

The role of an existential quantifier here points to a new direction of concern. For its invocation serves to indicate that there is yet another mode of "existence" that is distinct from any of the preceding. Or, again, consider the following cognate case:

There is a possible world w (again, presumably a *merely* possible one, which could have been actual, but is not) such that the condition Ξ is met by w: $(Ew)\Xi(w)$.

In all such cases, the mode of "existence" at issue is patently not real or actual existence, but only what might be called *genus-relative* existence (*sui generis* existence). Some suitable category of items (Γ) is presupposed and a correlative existential quantifier adopted that is devoid of any implication of *real* existence. We introduce a mode of quantification $\mathscr{E}$ correlative with Γ-membership and launch into a corresponding mode of "existence" by the generic formula:

$$E!\alpha \quad \text{iff} \quad (\mathscr{E}\beta)(\beta = \alpha)$$

A group of items is stipulated or postulated as a *range of discussion*—the "universe of discourse" or some sector of it—and the existence at issue is simply membership in this range, a conception devoid of any implications of *real* existence.

Here "existence" answers to the Quinean conception of ontological commitment of the formula "To be is to be the value of a [bound] variable."[13] Some group of items is specified as the range of objects under discussion (be they "possible worlds" or "mythic heroes" or "winged horses") and "existence" is simply membership in the group at issue. And this group need not consist of "things" in any plausible sense of this very flexible term; it may, for example, be moments of time or positions in space, or propositions, or numerical indices that are at issue.[14] To grant *this* sort of existence does not in fact commit us to holding that the items at issue *exist* at all, but just to holding that we can talk meaningfully about them. (It is something of a "Speak of the devil and up he pops" kind of existence.)

[13] W. V. Quine, "Designation and Existence," *The Journal of Philosophy*, vol. 36 (1939), pp. 701–709.
[14] Compare the author's essay on "Nonstandard Quantificational Logic" in his *Topics in Philosophical Logic* (Dordrecht, 1968), pp. 162–181.

Here we confront a mode of "existence" which abstains from any and all claims to real or actual *existence*. Rather than having a vehicle to "ontological commitment" as such, we have what is in fact a vehicle for ontological *evasion*. The standard disclaimer is in order that "any reference to *real* existents is purely coincidental."

VI. *Summary*

At this stage we have come to distinguish a fair plurality of significantly distinct senses of "exists":

(i) The actual existence of particulars as (contingent) members of the real world: E! iff $(\exists y)(y = x)$.

(ii) The OF-correlative existence of ground-level universals, such as the properties (relations, etc.) of particulars—be they actual or merely possible: E!ϕ iff $\Diamond(\exists x)\phi x$ iff $(\Sigma y)\phi y$.

(iii) The OF-correlative existence of higher-level universals with respect to lower-level ones or to particulars (thus representing the properties, relations, etc., which obtain among them): E!ϕ iff $(\exists\psi)[\phi(\psi)$ & $T(\psi)]$, where T is a suitable type-condition.

(iv) The OF-correlative existence of the dispositional properties of individuals and the lawful relationships among their properties (be they dispositional or absolute). The explication at issue here is analogous with case (ii), but involves a recourse to *physical* rather *logico-conceptual* modalities.

(v) The genus-relative "existence" of the stipulated (or assumed, or postulated) members of a universe of discourse: E!α iff $(\mathscr{E}\beta)(\beta = \phi)$.

A close analysis of the meaning of these several modes of existence accordingly shows them to be distinct and variegated. They do not share a common explication: indeed few common conceptual factors are present all along the line, apart from some mode or other of "existential quantification"—but existential quantification that is of various sorts and functions rather differently in the various cases. No common *meaning*—no common claim or contention—is uniformly present throughout. The several senses of "exists" are linked together—at best—by a set of family resemblances. We arrive at the upshot that *existence* is, in the end, an emphatically equivocal conception.

VII. *Methodology*

A word about methodology is in order. Throughout, this discussion has explored the prospects of a *uniform* construction or interpretation of the notion of existence across the range of its ontologically relevant applications. The exercise is one of attempted *reduction*, subject to the controlling question: Can all these uses of "exists" be explicated with the same body of conceptual machinery. Now, to be sure, in a way this can indeed *always* be done. For one can determine the *omnium-gatherum* class of existing things **E** by whatever set of membership criteria may be deemed appropriate, and then adopt the stipulation:

$$E!X \quad \text{iff} \quad (\exists Y)[Y \in \mathbf{E} \ \& \ Y = X]$$

This obviously produces a unified treatment. But it is also a purely formal unification—indeed a trivialization. The "explication" is useless because it affords no conceivable explanatory clarification. All the needed explications are *presupposed* in invoking the family of existential criteria that determine membership in **E**. The whole question is now simply transposed into this question of **E**-membership and the pivotal issue is just exactly what belongs to **E**.

Any attempt at rational reconstruction in philosophy calls for a substantiating cost-benefit analysis. One must balance its advantages (in point of such factors as simplicity, explanatory power, effective reduction of merely seeming diversity, etc.) against its disadvantages (distortion, oversimplification, or loss in point of some advantage akin to the preceding).

The uniformized "explication" of existence we have just envisaged in fact fails to meet the test of such a cost-benefit analysis. It makes no positive contribution to the enterprise of explanatory clarification—it obscures rather than illuminates the issues.

VIII. *Consequences*

Our analysis thus indicates the lack of any workable uniform conception to provide a covering umbrella for all these modes of existence. The philosophical study of existence—*ontology*—emerges from these considerations as a complex and internally diversified issue. No simple synoptic formula—such as Quine's well-known thesis "to be is to be the value of a variable"—is adequate to this ramified and variegated issue.

Despite this diversity, the logical analysis of the modes and modalities of existence is nevertheless a useful undertaking. For unless one becomes clear as to the composition of the concepts at issue, it is not possible to explore profitably their philosophical ramifications and interrelationships. Insofar as philosophy is a matter of the cost-benefit analysis of the pros and cons of various theoretical positions—as indeed it is, in large measure—the exploration of logico-conceptual distinctions of the sort we have dealt with here can play a useful role in the philosophical enterprise.

Nominalism is a particularly straightforward case in point. For the·nominalist (or at any rate the most prominent sort of nominalist), universals are no more than collection-principles for the assembling of suitably resembling *actualia*. Now the present deliberations have made it clear both what the commitments of this position are and what difficulties they encounter. For if universals are no more than points of resemblance among actually existing things, then it follows at once that the only properties that exist (really and genuinely *exist*—in the solely here-appropriate sense of the term) are those properties which are actually exemplified by reals. The consequences of the position abolish the line of distinction between property *existence* and property *exemplification*. An analysis of the consequences of the position make it easy to see what difficulties it encounters. Think again of such examples as Hume's missing shade of blue, the toothy smile of the Cheshire cat, or the unrealized values of parametrized properties (like height, weight, or temperature). All these now disappear as real (i.e., existing) properties. An analytical scrutiny of existence concepts shows that such a nominalism proposes on philosophico-ideological grounds (e.g., "economy" or "simplicity," etc.) to legislate a narrower range of alternatives than "the logic of the case" strictly requires. The present considerations suggest that this doctrine enjoins upon us an ontological posture that is in fact *smaller* than life.[15]

University of Pittsburgh

[15] The paper has profited from comments of my Pittsburgh colleague Gerald J. Massey on a draft version.

Index of Names

DATE DUE			